ON TYRANNY

AN INTERPRETATION OF XENOPHON'S

HIERO

By
LEO STRAUSS

With a Foreword by
ALVIN JOHNSON

The Free Press
Glencoe
Illinois

POLITICAL SCIENCE CLASSICS

Naphtaly Levy, *Editor*

John C. Calhoun

A DISQUISITION ON GOVERNMENT

Leo Strauss

ON TYRANNY

In preparation:

Montesquieu

SPIRIT OF LAWS

With this volume POLITICAL SCIENCE CLASSICS presents the first in a series of analytical works which will be a companion to the reprints of classic works in political science.

To
CWM

ON XENOPHON AND DR. STRAUSS

One who reads Montaigne's "Essays" will be struck by the freshness of his innumerable quotations from the Latin and Greek scholars. No scholar of today, except perhaps Gilbert Murray, could present so vivid a sense of the wisdom and wit of a civilization which in many respects has not been surpassed.

Much learning has been devoted to the classics in the last two hundred years. Too much learning, for philological analysis, philosophic, esthetic, and historic criticism have raised a great cloud of dust between the reader and the classical author. To Montaigne and Erasmus the writers of antiquity were essentially contemporary, to be read and enjoyed like good contemporary writers. Imagine the astonishment with which Erasmus would examine a huge octavo of the text and commentary of Tacitus, "Dialogus de Oratoribus." The essay of Tacitus can be read and enjoyed in an hour. The commentary, six hundred pages of fine print, can be half-mastered in a four-months seminar. No one who has ground through the commentary can enjoy the essay until many years have gone and the mental bruises left by the commentary have healed over.

The excessive learning of the last centuries has not only made dead literatures, as well as dead languages, out of Latin and Greek. It has introduced rankings in its necrology. Plato and Aristotle, Demosthenes and Cicero, Thucydides and Tacitus, Aeschylus and Sophocles, rank high. These are excellent gold mines for commentary virtuosity. Who reads Seneca, Montaigne's favorite author? Who reads Xenophon, much admired by the Hellenists of the Renaissance?

It was my good fortune, after a brief slavery in classical scholarship, to escape into the logomachies of economic theory. For relief I often turn to the classical authors. Having no responsibility to classical scholarship, I turn to what I like. I like Seneca and Xenophon.

I think of Xenophon as the first American, who, like the American looks "with keen untroubled gaze, home to the instant heart of things." Xenophon and the Americans are often charged with superficiality, because we are eye-minded and fail to see the things that aren't there. And indeed, as a wide-awake young fellow, Xenophon managed to get into the presence of Socrates, but got little that was Socratic out of his encounters. But he was blithe and gallant and resourceful. In his speech to the depressed Ten Thousand, after their generals had been murdered by treachery, he assured the Greeks they had nothing to fear from the million soldiers Artaxerxes had brought against them. But he had observed the long-limbed daughters of Mesopotamia, and he feared that if the Ten Thousand did not hurry away, they would become as the lotus eaters, forgetting their beloved fatherland.

Doesn't that sound like a Yankee?

The similarity of the Greek and the American is not to be pushed too far. The Greeks had no Bill of Rights; what might happen to a man who spoke freely is indicated by the fate of Socrates. Much Greek writing assumes mystical and allegorical form, unintelligible to the fatal uninitiate mob. But if the Greek tongue and pen were curbed, the Greek mind was extraordinarily free. We Americans can speak and write freely (within limits) but how about our minds?

At the time of the classic Greek writers the Devil had not been invented to tempt the unwary. No Greek had ever heard of the virtue of closed ears. While the Devil has been abolished from the equipment of cultivated Americans, various fears originating in the menace of the Tempter still lodge fast in our minds. Of these the most formidable is fear of propaganda. I, as a good American, could not bring myself to read Mrs. Lindbergh's "Wave of the Future." I was morally bound to close my ears to anything that could be said in favor of National Socialism. Xenophon could write sympathetically of Cyrus, the great menace to Hellenic freedom, and no Greek was ever warned to refrain

VIII

from reading the "Cyropaedia." For not only was the Greek unacquainted with the concept of the Tempter, but he had never heard of propaganda as an art. That remained for the Romans to invent and to develop majestically in the Augustan Age.

Like most Greeks, Xenophon was curious about other men's lives, whether a man in a given station enjoyed true happiness. What indeed was true happiness? Xenophon speculated on the point, but no more than an American did he break his head on it. He wanted pragmatic answers, not nebulous ultimacies.

Many years ago I read Xenophon's dialogue on tyranny. I was not then wholly emancipated from classical scholarship, and set the dialogue down as only faintly interesting. My friend and colleague, Dr. Strauss, has shown me how superficial my judgment was. The dialogue not only merits reading, but painstaking and sympathetic study.

I often marvel at Dr. Strauss. He is a scholar of the scholars. Yet his approach to a classical author is as direct as that of Erasmus or Montaigne. To Dr. Strauss Xenophon is a contemporary, more of a contemporary than many a statesman of our Sunny South. Xenophon does not need to be placed in his historic setting, explained anthropologically and politically. Dr. Strauss wants to know what is in Xenophon's mind; why does he raise one question and fail to raise another; what intellectual results he attains.

It is my hope that this essay may mark a new direction in classical scholarship, a systematic effort to excavate the classical authors from the successive strata of ashen scholarship and win back for us the original freshness and splendor of a great literature.

ALVIN JOHNSON

TABLE OF CONTENTS

"*The habit of writing against the government had, of itself, an unfavorable effect on the character. For whoever was in the habit of writing against the government was in the habit of breaking the law; and the habit of breaking even an unreasonable law tends to make men altogether lawless. . . .*

"*From the day on which the emancipation of our literature was accomplished, the purification of our literature began. . . . During a hundred and sixty years the liberty of our press has been constantly becoming more and more entire; and during those hundred and sixty years the restraint imposed on writers by the general feeling of readers has been constantly becoming more and more strict. . . . At this day foreigners, who dare not print a word reflecting on the government under which they live, are at a loss to understand how it happens that the freest press in Europe is the most prudish.*"

Macaulay

XIII

INTRODUCTION

It is proper that I should indicate my reasons for submitting this detailed analysis of a forgotten dialogue on tyranny to the consideration of political scientists.

Tyranny is a danger coeval with political life. The analysis of tyranny is therefore as old as political science itself. The analysis of tyranny that was made by the first political scientists was so clear, so comprehensive, and so unforgettably expressed that it was remembered and understood by generations which did not have any direct experience of actual tyranny. On the other hand, when we were brought face to face with tyranny—with a kind of tyranny that surpassed the boldest imagination of the most powerful thinkers of the past—our political science failed to recognize it. It is not surprising then that many of our contemporaries, disappointed or repelled by present-day analyses of present-day tyranny, were relieved when they rediscovered the pages in which Plato and other classical thinkers seemed to have interpreted for us the horrors of the twentieth century. What is surprising is that the renewed general interest in authentic interpretation of the phenomenon of tyranny did not lead to renewed interest, general or scholarly, in the only writing of the classical period which is explicitly devoted to the discussion of tyranny and its implications, and to nothing else, and which has never been subjected to comprehensive analysis: Xenophon's *Hiero*.

Not much observation and reflection is needed to realize that there is an essential difference between the tyranny analyzed by the classics and that of our age. In contradistinction to classical tyranny, present-day tyranny has at its disposal "technology" as well as "ideologies"; more generally expressed, it presupposes the existence of "science," i.e., of a particular interpretation, or kind, of science. Conversely, classical tyranny, unlike modern tyranny, was confronted, actually or potentially, by a science which was

1

not meant to be applied to "the conquest of nature" or to be popularized and diffused. But in noting this one implicitly grants that one cannot understand modern tyranny in its specific character before one has understood the elementary and in a sense natural form of tyranny which is pre-modern tyranny. This basic stratum of modern tyranny remains, for all practical purposes, unintelligible to us if we do not have recourse to the political science of the classics.

It is no accident that present-day political science has failed to grasp tyranny as what it really is. Our political science is haunted by the belief that "value judgments" are inadmissible in scientific considerations, and to call a régime tyrannical clearly amounts to pronouncing a "value judgment." The political scientist who accepts this view of science will speak of the mass-state, of dictatorship, of totalitarianism, of authoritarianism, and so on, and as a citizen he may wholeheartedly condemn these things; but as a political scientist he is forced to reject the notion of tyranny as "mythical." One cannot overcome this limitation without reflecting on the basis, or the origin, of present-day political science. Present-day political science often traces its origin to Machiavelli. There is truth in this contention. To say nothing of broader considerations, Machiavelli's *Prince* (as distinguished from his *Discourses on Livy*) is characterized by the deliberate indifference to the distinction between king and tyrant; the *Prince* presupposes the tacit rejection of that traditional distinction.[1] Machiavelli was fully aware that by conceiving the view expounded in the *Prince* he was breaking away from the whole tradition of political science; or, to apply to the *Prince* an expression which he uses when speaking of his *Discourses*, that he was taking a road which had not yet been followed by anyone.[2] To understand the basic premise of present-day political science, one would have to understand the meaning of the epoch-making change effected by Machiavelli; for that change consisted in the discovery of the continent on which all specifically modern political thought, and hence especially present-day political science, is at home.

It is precisely when trying to bring to light the deepest roots of modern political thought that one will find it to be very useful, not to say indispensable, to devote some attention to the *Hiero*. One cannot understand the meaning of Machiavelli's achievement if one does not confront his teaching with the traditional teaching which he rejects. As regards the *Prince* in particular, which is deservedly his most famous work, one has to confront its teaching with that of the traditional mirrors of princes. But in doing this one must beware of the temptation to try to be wiser, or rather more learned, than Machiavelli wants his readers to be, by attaching undue importance to medieval and early modern mirrors of princes which Machiavelli never stoops to mention by name. Instead one should concentrate on the only mirror of princes to which he emphatically refers and which is, as one would expect, the classic and the fountainhead of this whole genre: Xenophon's *Education of Cyrus.*[3] This work has never been studied by modern historians with even a small fraction of the care and concentration which it merits and which is needed if it is to disclose its meaning. The *Education of Cyrus* may be said to be devoted to the perfect king in contradistinction to the tyrant, whereas the *Prince* is characterized by the deliberate disregard of the difference between king and tyrant. There is only one earlier work on tyranny to which Machiavelli emphatically refers: Xenophon's *Hiero.*[4] The analysis of the *Hiero* leads to the conclusion that the teaching of that dialogue comes as near to the teaching of the *Prince* as the teaching of any Socratic could possibly come. By confronting the teaching of the Prince with that transmitted through the *Hiero,* one can grasp most clearly the subtlest and indeed the decisive difference between Socratic political science and Machiavellian political science. If it is true that all pre-modern political science rests on the foundations laid by Socrates, whereas all specifically modern political science rests on the foundations laid by Machiavelli, one may also say that the *Hiero* marks the point of closest contact between pre-modern and modern political science.[5]

As regards the manner in which I have treated my subject, I have been mindful that there are two opposed ways in which one can study the thought of the past. Many present-day scholars start from the historicist assumption, namely, that all human thought is "historical" or that the foundations of human thought are laid by specific experiences which are not, as a matter of principle, coeval with human thought as such. Yet there is a fatal disproportion between historicism and true historical understanding. The goal of the historian of thought is to understand the thought of the past "as it really has been," i.e., to understand it as exactly as possible as it was actually understood by its authors. But the historicist approaches the thought of the past on the basis of the historicist assumption which was wholly alien to the thought of the past. He is therefore compelled to attempt to understand the thought of the past better than it understood itself before he has understood it exactly as it understood itself. In one way or the other, his presentation will be a questionable mixture of interpretation and critique. It is the beginning of historical understanding, its necessary and, one is tempted to add, its sufficient condition that one realizes the problematic character of historicism. For one cannot realize it without becoming seriously interested in an impartial confrontation of the historicist approach that prevails today with the non-historicist approach of the past. And such a confrontation in its turn requires that the non-historicist thought of the past be understood on its own terms, and not in the way in which it presents itself within the horizon of historicism.

In accordance with this principle, I have tried to understand Xenophon's thought as exactly as I could. I have not tried to relate his thought to his "historical situation" because this is not the natural way of reading the work of a wise man and, in addition, Xenophon never indicated that he wanted to be understood that way. I assumed that Xenophon, being an able writer, gave us to the best of his powers the information required for understanding his work. I have relied therefore as much as possible on what he himself says, directly or indirectly, and as little as possible on extraneous information, to say nothing of modern hypotheses. Distrustful of all conventions, however trivial, which are likely to do harm to matters of importance, I went so far as to omit the angular brackets with which modern scholars are in the habit of adorning their citations of certain ancient writings. It goes without saying that I never believed that my mind was moving in a larger "circle of ideas" than Xenophon's mind.

The neglect of the *Hiero* (as well as of the *Education of Cyrus*) is no doubt partly due to the fashionable underestimation and even contempt of Xenophon's intellectual powers. Until the end of the eighteenth century, he was generally considered a wise man and a classic in the precise sense. In the nineteenth and twentieth centuries, he is compared as a philosopher to Plato, and found wanting; he is compared as a historian to Thucydides, and found wanting. One need not, as well one might, take issue with the views of philosophy and of history which are presupposed in these comparisons. One merely has to raise the question whether Xenophon wanted to be understood primarily as a philosopher or as a historian. In the manuscripts of his works, he is frequently designated as "the orator Xenophon." It is reasonable to assume that the temporary eclipse of Xenophon—just as the temporary eclipse of Livy and of Cicero—has been due to a decline in the understanding of the significance of rhetoric: both the peculiar "idealism" and the peculiar "realism" of the nineteenth century were guided by the modern concept of "Art" and for that reason were unable to understand the crucial significance of the lowly art of rhetoric. While they could thus find a place for Plato and Thucydides, they completely failed duly to appreciate Xenophon.

Xenophon's rhetoric is not ordinary rhetoric; it is Socratic rhetoric. The character of Socratic rhetoric does not become sufficiently clear from the judiciously scattered remarks on the subject that occur in Plato's and Xenophon's writings, but only from detailed analyses of its products. The most perfect product of Socratic rhetoric is the dialogue. The form of Plato's dialogues has been frequently discussed, but no one would claim that the problem of the Platonic dialogue has been solved. Modern analyses are, as a rule, vitiated by the estheticist prejudice of the interpreters. Yet Plato's expulsion of the poets from his best city should have sufficed for discouraging any estheticist approach. It would seem that the attempt to clarify the meaning of the dialogue should start from an analysis of Xenophon's dialogue. Xenophon uses far fewer devices than Plato uses even in his simplest works. By understanding the art of Xenophon, one will realize certain minimum requirements that one must fulfill when interpreting any

Platonic dialogue, requirements which today are so little fulfilled that they are hardly known.

The dialogue that deserves the name communicates the thought of the author in an indirect or oblique way. Thus the danger of arbitrary interpretation might well seem to be overwhelming. The danger can be overcome only if the greatest possible attention is paid to every detail, and especially to the unthematic details, and if the function of Socratic rhetoric is never lost sight of.

Socratic rhetoric is meant to be an indispensable instrument of philosophy. Its purpose is to lead potential philosophers to philosophy both by training them and by liberating them from the charms which obstruct the philosophic effort, as well as to prevent the access to philosophy of those who are not fit for it. Socratic rhetoric is emphatically just. It is animated by the spirit of social responsibility. It is based on the premise that there is a disporportion between the intransigent quest for truth and the requirements of society, or that not all truths are always harmless. Society will always try to tyrannize thought. Socratic rhetoric is the classic means for ever again frustrating these attempts. This highest kind of rhetoric did not die with the immediate pupils of Socrates. Many monographs bear witness to the fact that great thinkers of later times have used a kind of caution or thrift in communicating their thought to posterity which is no longer appreciated: it ceased to be appreciated at about the same time at which historicism emerged, at about the end of the eighteenth century.

The experience of the present generation has taught us to read the great political literature of the past with different eyes and with different expectations. The lesson may not be without value for our political orientation. We are now brought face to face with a tyranny which holds out the threat of becoming, thanks to "the conquest of nature" and in particular of human nature, what no earlier tyranny ever became: perpetual and universal. Confronted by the appalling alternative that man, or human thought, must be collectivized either by one stroke and without mercy or else by slow and gentle processes, we are forced to wonder how we could escape from this dilemma. We reconsider therefore the elementary and unobtrusive conditions of human freedom.

The historical form in which this reflection is here presented is perhaps not inappropriate. The manifest and deliberate collectivization or co-ordination of thought is being prepared in a hidden and frequently quite unconscious way by the spread of the teaching that all human thought is collective independently of any human effort directed to this end, because all human thought is historical. There seems to be no more appropriate way of combating this teaching than the study of history.

As has been indicated, one must have some patience if one wants to grasp the meaning of the *Hiero*. The patience of the interpreter does not make superfluous the patience of the reader of the interpretation. In explaining writings like the *Hiero,* one has to engage in long-winded and sometimes repetitious considerations which can arrest attention only if one sees their purpose, and it is necessary that this purpose should reveal itself in its proper place, which cannot be at the beginning. If one wants to establish the precise meaning of a subtle hint, one must proceed in a way which comes dangerously close to the loathsome business of explaining a joke. The charm produced by Xenophon's unobtrusive art is destroyed, at least for a moment, if that art is made obtrusive by the interpretation. Still, I believe that I have not dotted all the i's. One can only hope that the time will again come when Xenophon's art will be understood by a generation which, properly trained in their youth, will no longer need cumbersome introductions like the present study.

I

THE PROBLEM

The intention of the *Hiero* is nowhere stated by the author. Being an account of a conversation between the poet Simonides and the tyrant Hiero, the work consists almost exclusively of the utterances, recorded in direct speech, of these two characters. The author limits himself to describing at the beginning in sixteen words the circumstances in which the conversation took place, and to linking with each other, or separating from each other, the statements of the two interlocutors by expressions such as "Simonides said" and "Hiero answered."

The intention of the work does not become manifest at once from the content. The work consists of two main parts of very unequal length, the first part making up about five-sevenths of the whole. In the first part (ch. 1-7), Hiero proves to Simonides that the life of a tyrant, as compared with the life of a private man, is so unhappy that the tyrant can hardly do better than to hang himself. In the second part (ch. 8-11), Simonides proves to Hiero that the tyrant could be the happiest of men. The first part seems to be directed against the popular prejudice that the life of a tyrant is more pleasant than private life. The second part, however, seems to establish the view that the life of a beneficent tyrant is superior, in the most important respect, to private life.[1] At first glance, the work as a whole clearly conveys the message that the life of a beneficent tyrant is highly desirable. But it is not clear what that message means since we do not know to what type of men it is addressed. If we assume that the work is addressed to tyrants, its intention is to exhort them to exercise their rule in a spirit of shrewd benevolence. Yet only a very small part of its readers can be supposed to be actual tyrants. The work as a whole may therefore have to be taken as a recommendation addressed to

8

properly equipped young men who are pondering what way of life they should choose—a recommendation to strive for tyrannical power, not indeed to gratify their desires, but to gain the love and admiration of all men by deeds of benevolence on the greatest possible scale.[2] Socrates, the teacher of Xenophon, was suspected of teaching his companions to be "tyrannical": [3] Xenophon lays himself open to the same suspicion.

Yet it is not Xenophon, but Simonides, who proves that a beneficent tyrant will reach the summit of happiness, and one cannot identify without further consideration the author's views with those of one of his characters. The fact that Simonides is called "wise" by Hiero [4] does not prove anything, since we do not know what Xenophon thought of Hiero's competence. But even if we assume that Simonides is simply the mouthpiece of Xenophon, great difficulties remain, for Simonides' thesis is ambiguous. It is addressed to a tyrant who is out of heart with tyranny, who has just declared that a tyrant can hardly do better than to hang himself. Does it not serve the purpose of comforting the sad tyrant, and does not the intention to comfort detract from the sincerity of a speech? [5] Is any speech addressed to a tyrant by a man who is in the tyrant's power, likely to be a sincere speech? [6]

II

THE TITLE AND THE FORM

While practically everything said in the *Hiero* is said by Xenophon's characters, Xenophon himself takes full responsibility for the title of the work.[1] The title is Ἱέρων ἤ Τυραννικός. No other work contained in the *Corpus Xenophonteum* has a title consisting of both a proper name and an adjective referring to the subject. The first part of the title is reminiscent of the title of the *Agesilaus*. The *Agesilaus* deals with an outstanding Greek king, just as the *Hiero* deals with an outstanding Greek tyrant. Proper names of individuals also occur in the titles of the *Cyri Institutio,* the *Cyri Expeditio,* and the *Apologia Socratis.* Agesilaus, the two Cyrus', and Socrates seem to be the men whom Xenophon admired most. But the two Cyrus' were not Greek, and Socrates was not a ruler: the *Agesilaus* and the *Hiero,* the only writings of Xenophon the titles of which contain proper names of individuals in the nominative, are the only writings of Xenophon which may be said to be devoted to Greek rulers.

The second part of the title reminds one of the titles of the *Hipparchicus,* the *Oeconomicus,* and the *Cynegeticus.* These three writings serve the purpose of teaching skills befitting gentlemen: the skill of a commander of cavalry, the skill of managing one's estate, and the skill of hunting.[2] Accordingly, one should expect that the purpose of the *Tyrannicus* is to teach the skill of the tyrant, the σοφία (or τέχνη) τυραννική;[3] and in fact Simonides does therein teach Hiero how best to exercise tyrannical rule.

There is only one work of Xenophon apart from the *Hiero* which has an alternative title: the Πόροι ἤ περὶ προσόδων (*"Ways and Means"*). The purpose of that work is to show the (democratic) rulers of Athens how they could become more just by showing them how they could overcome the necessity under

10

which they found themselves of acting unjustly.[4] That is to say, its purpose is to show how the democratic order of Athens could be improved without being fundamentally changed. Similarly, Simonides shows the tyrannical ruler of Syracuse how he could overcome the necessity of acting unjustly under which he found himself without abandoning tyrannical rule as such.[5] Xenophon, the pupil of Socrates, seems to have considered both democracy and tyranny faulty régimes.[6] The *Ways and Means* and the *Hiero* are the only works of Xenophon which are devoted to the question of how a given political order ($\pi o \lambda \iota \tau \epsilon \acute{\iota} \alpha$) of a faulty character could be corrected without being transformed into a good political order.

Xenophon could easily have explained in direct terms the conditional character of the policy recommended in the *Hiero*. Had he done so, however, he might have conveyed the impression that he was not absolutely opposed to tyranny. But "the cities," and especially Athens, were absolutely opposed to tyranny.[7] Besides, one of the charges brought against Socrates was that he taught his pupils to be "tyrannical." Reasons such as these explain why Xenophon presented his reflections on the improvement of tyrannical rule (and therewith on the stabilization of such rule), as distinguished from his reflections on the improvement of the Athenian régime, in the form of a dialogue in which he does not participate in any way: the *Hiero* is the only work of Xenophon in which the author, when speaking in his own name, never uses the first person, whereas the *Ways and Means* is the only work of Xenophon whose very opening word is an emphatic "I." The reasons indicated explain besides why the fairly brief suggestions for the improvement of tyrannical rule are prefaced by a considerably more extensive discourse which expounds the undesirable character of tyranny in the strongest possible terms.

The *Hiero* consists almost exclusively of utterances of men other than the author. There is only one other work of Xenophon which has that character: the *Oeconomicus*. In the *Oeconomicus*, too, the author "hides himself" [8] almost completely. The *Oeconomicus* is a dialogue between Socrates and another Athenian on the management of the household. According to Socrates, there does not seem to be an essential difference between the art of managing

the household and that of managing the affairs of the city: both
are called by him "the royal art." [9] Hence, it can only be due to
secondary considerations that the dialogue which is destined to
teach that art is called *Oeconomicus,* and not *Politicus* or *Basilicus.*
There is ample evidence to show that the *Oeconomicus,* while
apparently devoted to the economic art only, actually deals with
the royal art as such.[10] It is then permissible to describe the relation of Xenophon's two dialogues as that of a *Basilicus* to a *Tyrannicus*: the two dialogues deal with *the* two types of monarchic
rule.[11] Since the economist is a ruler, the *Oeconomicus* is, just as
the *Hiero,* a dialogue between a wise man (Socrates) [12] and a ruler
(the potential economist Critobulus and the actual economist
Ischomachus). But whereas the wise man and the rulers of the
Oeconomicus are Athenians, the wise man and the ruler of the
Hiero are not. And whereas the wise man and the potential ruler
of the *Oeconomicus* were friends of Xenophon, and Xenophon
himself was present at their conversation, the wise man and the
ruler of the *Hiero* were dead long before Xenophon's time. It was
evidently impossible to assign the "tyrannical" teaching to Socrates.
But the reason was not that there was any scarcity of actual or
potential tyrants in the entourage of Socrates. Rather the reverse.
Nothing would have been easier for Xenophon than to arrange a
conversation on how to rule well as a tyrant between Socrates and
Charmides or Critias [13] or Alcibiades. So doing, though—giving
Socrates such a role in such a context—he would have destroyed
the basis of his own defense of Socrates. It is for this reason that
the place occupied in the *Oeconomicus* by Socrates is occupied
in the *Hiero* by another wise man. After having chosen Simonides,
Xenophon was free to present him as engaged in a conversation
with the Athenian tyrant Hipparchus; [14] but he apparently wished
to avoid any connection between the topics "tyranny" and
"Athens."

One cannot help wondering why Xenophon chose Simonides
as a chief character in preference to certain other wise men who
were known to have conversed with tyrants.[15] A clue is offered
by the parallelism between the *Hiero* and the *Oeconomicus.* The
royal art is morally superior to the tyrannical art. Socrates, who

teaches the royal or economic art, has perfect self-control as regards the pleasures deriving from wealth.[16] Simonides, who teaches
the tyrannical art, was famous for his greed.[17] Socrates, who
teaches the economic or royal art, was not himself an economist
because he was not interested in increasing his property; accordingly, his teaching consists largely of giving to a potential economist an account of a conversation which he once had with an
actual economist.[18] Simonides, who teaches the tyrannical art,
and therewith at least some rudiments of the economic art as
well,[19] without any assistance, *was* an "economist."

In the light of the parallelism between the *Oeconomicus* and
the *Hiero*, our previous explanation of the fact that Xenophon
presented the "tyrannical" teaching in the form of a dialogue
proves to be insufficient. With a view to that parallelism, we have
to raise the more comprehensive question as to why the *Oeconomicus* and the *Hiero*, as distinguished from Xenophon's two other
technical writings, the *Hipparchicus* and the *Cynegeticus*, are
written in the form, not of treatises, nor even of stories, but of
dialogues. The subjects of the two former works, we shall ven-
ture to say, are of a higher order, or are more philosophic than
those of the two latter. Accordingly, their treatment too should
be more philosophic. From Xenophon's point of view, philosophic
treatment is conversational treatment. Conversational teaching of
the skill of ruling has these two particular advantages. First, it
necessitates the confrontation of a wise man (the teacher) and a
ruler (the pupil). Besides, it compels the reader to wonder whether
the lessons given by the wise man to the ruler bore fruit, because it
compels the author to leave unanswered that question which is
nothing less than a special form of the fundamental question of
the relation of theory and practice, or of knowledge and virtue.

The second advantage of conversational teaching is particularly striking in the *Hiero*. Whereas the proof of the unhappiness
of the unjust tyrant is emphatically based on experience,[20] the
proof of the happiness of the beneficent tyrant is not: that happiness is merely promised—by a poet. The reader is left wondering
whether experience offered a single instance of a tyrant who was
happy because he was virtuous.[21] The corresponding question

forced upon the reader of the *Oeconomicus* is answered, if not by the *Oeconomicus* itself, by the *Cyropaedia* and the *Agesilaus*. But the question of the actual happiness of the virtuous tyrant is left open by the *Corpus Xenophonteum* as a whole. And whereas the *Cyropaedia* and the *Agesilaus* set the happiness of the virtuous kings Cyrus and Agesilaus beyond any imaginable doubt by show- ing or at least intimating how they died, the *Hiero,* owing to its form, cannot throw any light on the end of the tyrant Hiero.[22]

We hope to have explained why Xenophon presents the "tyrannical" teaching in the form of a conversation between Simonides and a non-Athenian tyrant. An adequate understand- ing of that teaching requires more than an understanding of its content. One must also consider the form in which it is presented, for otherwise one cannot realize the place which it occupies, ac- cording to the author, within the whole of wisdom. The form in which it is presented characterizes it as a philosophic teaching of the sort that a truly wise man would not care to present in his own name. Moreover, by throwing some light on the procedure of the wise man who stoops to present the "tyrannical" teaching in his own name, i.e., of Simonides, the author shows us how that teaching should be presented to its ultimate addressee, the tyrant.

III

THE SETTING

a. The characters and their intentions

"Simonides the poet came once upon a time to Hiero the tyrant. After both had found leisure, Simonides said. . . ." This is all that Xenophon says thematically and explicitly about the situation in which the conversation took place. "Simonides came to Hiero": Hiero did not come to Simonides. Tyrants do not like to travel to foreign parts,[1] and, as Simonides seems to have said to Hiero's wife, the wise are spending their time at the doors of the rich and not *vice versa*.[2] Simonides came to Hiero "once upon a time": he was merely visiting Hiero; those coming to display before the tyrant something wise or beautiful or good prefer to go away as soon as they have received their reward.[3] The conversation opens "after both had found leisure" and, we may add, when they were alone: it does not open immediately on Simonides' arrival. It appears in the course of the conversation that prior to the conversation Hiero had acquired a definite opinion of Simonides' qualities, and Simonides had made some observations about Hiero. It is not impossible that the business which each had before both found leisure was a business which they had with each other. At any rate, they were not complete strangers to each other at the moment when the conversation starts. Their knowledge of, or their opinions about, each other might even explain why they engage in a leisurely conversation at all, as well as how they behave during their conversation from its very beginning.

It is Simonides who opens the conversation. What is his purpose? He starts with the question, whether Hiero would be willing to explain to him something which he is likely to know better than the poet. The polite question which he addresses to

15

a tyrant who is not his ruler, keeps in the appropriate middle between the informal request, so frequently used by Socrates in particular, "Tell me," or the polite request, "I want very much to learn," on the one hand, and the deferential question addressed by Socrates to tyrants who were his rulers (the "legislators" Critias and Charicles), "Is it permitted to inquire. . .?" on the other.[4] By his question, Simonides presents himself as a wise man who, always desirous to learn, wishes to avail himself of the opportunity of learning something from Hiero. He thus assigns to Hiero the position of a man who is, in a certain respect, wiser, a greater authority than he is himself. Hiero, fully aware of how wise Simonides is, has not the slightest notion as to what sort of thing he could know better than a man of Simonides' wisdom. Simonides explains to him that since he, Hiero, was born a private man and is now a tyrant, he is, on the basis of his experience of both conditions, likely to know better than Simonides in what way the life of a tyrant and that of private men differ with regard to human enjoyments and pains.[5] The choice of the topic is perfect. A comparison of a tyrant's life and private life is the only comprehensive, or "wise," topic in the discussion of which a wise man can with some plausibility be presented as inferior to a tyrant who once had been a private man and who is not wise. Moreover, the point of view which, as Simonides suggests, should guide the comparison—pleasure-pain as distinguished from virtue-vice—seems to be characteristic of tyrants as distinguished from kings.[6] Simonides seems then to open the conversation with the intention of learning something from Hiero, or of getting some first-hand information from an authority on the subject which he proposes.

Yet the reason with which he justifies his question in the eyes of Hiero is only a probable one. It leaves out of consideration the decisive contribution of judgment, or wisdom, to the correct evaluation of experiences.[7] Moreover, the question itself is not of such a nature that peculiar experiences which a wise man may or may not have had (such as those which only an actual tyrant can have had) could contribute significantly to its complete answer. It rather belongs to the kind of question to which the wise man as such (and only the wise man as such) necessarily possesses the complete answer. Simonides' question concerning the manner of difference between the tyrant's life and private life in regard to pleasures and pains is identical, in the context, with the question as to which of the two ways of life is more desirable; for "pleasure-pain" is the only ultimate criterion of preference which is thematically considered. The initial question is rendered more specific by the assertion which Simonides makes soon afterwards that the tyrant's life knows many more pleasures of all kinds and many fewer pains of all kinds than private life, in other words, that tyrannical life is more desirable than private life.[8] Even Hiero states that Simonides' assertion is surprising in the mouth of a reputedly wise man: a wise man should be able to judge of the happiness or misery of the tyrant's life without ever having had the actual experience of tyrannical life.[9] The question as to whether, or how far, tyrannical life is more desirable than private life, and in particular whether, or how far, it is more desirable from the point of view of pleasure, is no longer a question for a man who has acquired wisdom.[10] If Simonides was a wise man, he must then have had a motive other than eagerness to learn, for inquiring with Hiero about that subject.

Hiero expresses the view that Simonides is a wise man, a man much wiser than he himself is. This assertion is borne out to a certain extent by the action of the dialogue, by which Simonides is shown to be able to teach Hiero the art of ruling as a tyrant. While Simonides is thus shown to be wiser than Hiero, it is by no means certain that Xenophon considered him simply wise. What Xenophon thought of Simonides' wisdom can be definitely established only by a comparison of Simonides with Socrates, whom Xenophon certainly considered wise. It is possible, however, to reach a provisional conclusion on the basis of the parallelism of the *Hiero* and the *Oeconomicus* as well as of the following consideration: If Simonides was wise, he had conversational skill, i.e., he could do what he liked with any interlocutor.[11] or he could lead any conversation to the end which he desired. His conversation with Hiero leads up to such suggestions about the improvement of tyrannical rule as a wise man could be expected to make to a tyrant towards whom he is well disposed. We shall then

assume that the wise Simonides opens the conversation intending
to be of some benefit to Hiero, perhaps in order to be benefited in
turn or to benefit the tyrant's subjects. During his stay with Hiero,
Simonides had observed several things about the ruler—some
concerning his appetite, some concerning his amours; [12] and
Simonides knew that Hiero was making certain grave mistakes, such
as his participating at the Olympian and Pythian games.[13] To
express this more generally, Simonides knew that Hiero was not a
perfect ruler. He decided to teach him how to rule well as a
tyrant. More specifically, he considered it advisable to warn him
against certain grave mistakes. But, to say nothing of common
politeness, no one wishes to rebuke, or to speak against, a tyrant
in his presence.[14] Simonides had, then, by the least offensive means
to reduce the tyrant to a mood in which the latter would be pleased
to listen attentively to, and even to ask for, the poet's advice. He
had at the same time, or by the same action, to convince Hiero of
his competence to give sound advice to a tyrant.

Before Simonides can teach Hiero how to rule as a tyrant, he
has to make him aware, or to remind him, of the difficulties with
which he is beset and which he cannot overcome, of the shortcomings of his rule, and indeed of his whole life. To be made aware
by someone else of one's own shortcomings means, for most people,
to be humbled by the censor. Simonides has to humble the
tyrant; he has to reduce him to a condition of inferiority; or, to
describe Simonides' intention in the light of the aim apparently
achieved by him, he has to dishearten the tyrant. Moreover, if
he intends to use Hiero's recognition of his shortcomings as the
starting point for his teaching, he has to induce Hiero expressly
to grant all the relevant unpleasant facts about his life. The least
he can do, in order to avoid unnecessary offense, is to talk, not
about Hiero's life, but about a more general, a less offensive, subject. To begin with, we shall assume that when starting a conversation with Hiero about the relative desirability of the life of the
tyrant and private life, he is guided by the intention to dishearten
the tyrant by a comparison of the life of the tyrant, and therewith
of Hiero's own life, with private life.

To reach this immediate aim in the least offensive manner,

Simonides has to create a situation in which, not he, but the tyrant himself, explains the shortcomings of his life, or of tyrannical life in general, and a situation in which, moreover, the tyrant does this normally unpleasant work, not only spontaneously, but even gladly. The artifice by means of which Simonides brings about this result consists in his giving to Hiero an opportunity of vindicating his superiority while demonstrating his inferiority. He starts the conversation by presenting himself explicitly as a man who has to learn from Hiero, or who is, in a certain respect, less wise than Hiero, or by assuming the role of the pupil. Thereafter, he makes himself the spokesman of the opinion that tyrannical life is more desirable than private life, i.e., of the crude opinion about tyranny which is characteristic of the unwise, of the multitude, or the vulgar.[15] He thus presents himself tacitly, and therefore all the more effectively, as a man who is absolutely less wise than Hiero. He thus tempts Hiero to assume the role of the teacher.[16] He succeeds in seducing him into refuting the vulgar opinion, and thus into proving that tyrannical life, and hence his own life, is extremely unhappy. Hiero vindicates his superiority by winning his argument, which, as far as its content is concerned, would be merely depressing for him: by proving that he is extremely unhappy, he proves that he is wiser than the wise Simonides. Yet his victory is his defeat. By appealing to the tyrant's interest in superiority, or desire for victory, Simonides brings about the tyrant's spontaneous and almost joyful recognition of all the shortcomings of his life and therewith a situation in which the offering of advice is the act, not of an awkward schoolmaster, but of a humane poet. And besides, in the moment that Hiero becomes aware of his having walked straight into the trap which Simonides had so ingeniously and so charmingly set for him, he will be more convinced than ever before of Simonides' wisdom.

Before Simonides starts teaching Hiero, in other words, in the largest part of the *Hiero* (ch. 1-7), he presents himself to Hiero as less wise than he really is. In the first part of the *Hiero,* Simonides hides his wisdom. He does not merely report the vulgar opinion about tyranny, he does not merely hand it over to Hiero for its refutation by asking him what he thinks about it; he actually adopts it. Hiero is justifiably under the impression that Simonides is ignorant of, or deceived about, the nature of tyrannical life.[17] Thus the question arises as to why Simonides' artifice does not defeat his purpose: why can Hiero still take him seriously? Why does he not consider him a fool, a foolish follower of the opinions of the vulgar? The situation in which the conversation takes place remains wholly obscure as long as this difficulty is not satisfactorily explained.

The difficulty would be insoluble if to be vulgar merely meant to be simply foolish or unwise. The vulgar opinion about tyranny can be summarized as follows: Tyranny is bad for the city but good for the tyrant, for the tyrannical life is the most enjoyable and desirable way of life.[18] This opinion is founded on the basic premise of the vulgar mind that bodily pleasures and wealth or power are more important than virtue. The vulgar opinion is contested, not only by the wise, but above all by the gentlemen. According to the opinion of the perfect gentleman, tyranny is bad, not only for the city, but above all for the tyrant himself.[19] By adopting the vulgar view, Simonides tacitly rejects the gentleman's view. Should he not be a gentleman? Should he lack the moderation, the self-restraint of the gentleman? Should he be dangerous? Whether this suspicion arises evidently depends on what opinion is held by Hiero about the relation of "wise" and "gentlemen." But if it arises, the theoretical and somewhat playful discussion will transform itself into a conflict.

The ironical element of Simonides' procedure would endanger the achievement of his serious purpose if it did not arouse a deeper emotion in the soul of the tyrant than the somewhat whimsical desire to win a dialectical victory. The manner in which he understands, and reacts to, Simonides' question and assertion is bound to be determined by his view of Simonides' qualities and of his intention. He considers Simonides a wise man. His attitude towards Simonides will then be a special case of his attitude towards wise men in general. He says that tyrants fear the wise. His attitude towards Simonides must be understood accordingly: "Instead of admiring" him, he fears him.[20] Considering the fact that Simonides is a stranger in Hiero's city, and therefore not likely to be really dangerous to Hiero's rule,[21] we prefer to say that his admiration for Simonides is mitigated by some fear, by some fear *in statu nascendi*, i.e., by distrust. He does not trust people in any case; he will be particularly distrustful in his dealings with a man of unusually great abilities. Hence he is not likely to be perfectly frank. He is likely to be as reserved as Simonides although for somewhat different reasons.[22] Their conversation is likely to take place in an atmosphere of limited straightforwardness.

The tyrant's fear of the wise is a specific one. This crucial fact is explained by Hiero in what is even literally the central passage of the *Hiero*.[23] He fears the brave because they might take risks for the sake of freedom. He fears the just because the multitude might desire to be ruled by them. As regards the wise, he fears that "they might contrive something." He fears, then, the brave and the just because their virtues or virtuous actions might bring about the restoration of freedom or at least of non-tyrannical government. This much, and not more, is explained by Hiero in unequivocal terms. He does not say explicitly what kind of danger he apprehends from the wise: Does he fear that they might contrive something for the sake of freedom or of just government, or does he fear that they might contrive something for some other purpose? [24] Hiero's explicit statement leaves unanswered the crucial question, Why does the tyrant fear the wise?

The most cautious explanation of Hiero's silence would be the suggestion that he does not know what the wise intend. Having once been a private man, a private citizen, a subject of a tyrant, he knows and understands the goals of the brave and the just as well as they themselves do. But he has never been a wise man: he does not know wisdom from his own experience. He realizes that wisdom is a virtue, a power, hence a limit to the tyrant's power, and therefore a danger to the tyrant's rule. He realizes, besides, that wisdom is something different from courage and justice. But he does not clearly grasp the specific and positive character of wisdom: wisdom is more elusive than courage and justice. Perhaps it would not be too much to say that for the tyrant wisdom, as distinguished from courage and justice, is something uncanny. At any rate, his fear of the wise is an indeterminate fear, in some cases (as in the case of Hiero's fear of Simonides) hardly more than a vague, but strong, uneasiness.

This attitude towards the wise is characteristic not only of tyrants. The fate of Socrates must be presumed always to have been present to Xenophon's mind. It confirmed the view that wise men are apt to be envied by men who are less wise or altogether unwise, and that they are exposed to all sorts of vague suspicion on the part of "the many." Xenophon himself suggested that the same experience which Socrates had had under a democracy could have been had by him under a monarchy: wise men are apt to be envied, or suspected, by monarchs as well as by ordinary citizens.[25] The distrust of the wise, which proceeds from lack of understanding of wisdom, is characteristic of the vulgar, of tyrants and non-tyrants alike. Hiero's attitude towards the wise bears at least some resemblance to the vulgar attitude.

The fate of Socrates showed that those who do not understand the nature of wisdom are apt to mistake the wise man for the sophist. Both the wise man and the sophist are in a sense possessors of wisdom. But whereas the sophist prostitutes wisdom for base purposes, and especially for money, the wise man makes the most noble or moral use of wisdom.[26] The wise man is a gentleman, whereas the sophist is servile. The error of mistaking the wise man for the sophist is made possible by the ambiguity of "gentlemanliness." In common parlance, "gentleman" designates a just and brave man, a good citizen, who as such is not necessarily a wise man. Ischomachus, that perfectly respectable man whom Xenophon confronts with Socrates, is called a gentleman by everyone, by men and women, by strangers and citizens. In the Socratic meaning of the term, the gentleman is identical with the wise man.[27] The essence of wisdom, or what distinguishes wisdom from ordinary gentlemanliness, escapes the vulgar, who may thus be led to believe in an opposition between wisdom and the only gentlemanliness known to them: they may doubt the gentlemanliness of the wise. They will see this much, that wisdom is the ability to contrive the acquisition of that possession which is most valuable and therefore most difficult to obtain. But believing that the tyrannical life is the most enjoyable and therefore the most desirable possession, they will be inclined to identify wisdom with the ability to become a tyrant or to remain a tyrant. Those who succeeded in acquiring tyrannical power, and in preserving it for ever so short a time, are admired as wise and lucky men: the specific ability which enables a man to become, and to remain, a tyrant is popularly identified with wisdom. On the other hand, if a wise man manifestly abstains from striving for tyrannical power, he may still be suspected of teaching his friends to be "tyrannical." [28] On the basis of the vulgar notion of wisdom, the conclusion is plausible that a wise man would aspire to tyranny or, if he is already a tyrant, that he would attempt to preserve his position.

Let us now return to Hiero's statement about the various types of human excellence. The brave would take risks for the sake of freedom; the just would be desired as rulers by the multitude. The brave as brave would not be desired as rulers, and the just as just would not rebel. As clearly as the brave as brave are distinguished from the just as just, the wise as wise are distinguished from both the brave and the just. Would the wise take risks for the sake of freedom? Did Socrates, as distinguished from Thrasybulus, take such risks? While blaming "somewhere" the practices of Critias and his fellows, and while refusing to obey their unjust commands, he did not work for their overthrow.[29] Would the wise be desired as rulers by the multitude? Was Socrates desired as a ruler by the multitude? One has no right to assume that Hiero's view of wisdom and justice is identical with Xenophon's. The context suggests that, according to Hiero, the wise as wise have a purpose different from those of the brave and of the just, or, if courage and justice combined are the essence of gentlemanliness, that the wise man is not necessarily a gentleman. The context suggests that the wise have another goal than the typical enemies of tyranny, who are concerned with restoring freedom and "possession of good laws." [30] This suggestion is far from being contradicted by Simonides, who avoids in his teaching the very terms "freedom" and "law." There is only one reasonable alternative: the tyrant fears the wise man because he might attempt to overthrow the tyrant, not in order to restore non-tyrannical government, but to become a tyrant himself, or because he might advise a pupil or friend of his as to how he could become a tyrant by overthrowing the actual tyrant. Hiero's central statement does not exclude but rather suggests the vulgar view of wisdom; [31] it does not exclude but rather suggests the view that the wise man is a potential tyrant.[32]

Hiero is somehow aware of the fact that wise men do not judge of happiness or misery on the basis of outward appearances because they know that the seat of happiness and misery is in the souls of men. It therefore seems surprising to him that Simonides should identify, for all practical purposes, happiness with wealth and power, and ultimately with the tyrannical life. He does not say, however, that Simonides, being a wise man, cannot possibly mean what he says, or that he must be joking. On the contrary, he takes Simonides' assertion most seriously. He does not consider it incredible or impossible that a wise man should hold the view adopted by Simonides.[33] He does not consider it impossible because he believes that only the experience of a tyrant can establish with final certainty whether tyrannical life is, or is not, more desirable than private life.[34] He does not really know the purpose of the wise. He is then not convinced that the wise man is a potential tyrant. Nor is he convinced of the contrary. He oscillates between two diametrically opposed views, between the vulgar view and the wise view of wisdom. Which of the two opposed views he will take in a given case will depend on the behavior of the wise individual with whom he converses. Regarding Simonides, the question is decided by the fact that he adopts the vulgar opinion according to which the tyrannical life is more desirable than private life. At least in his conversation with Simonides, Hiero will be disturbed by the suspicion that the wise man may be a potential tyrant, or a potential adviser of possible rivals of Hiero.[35]

Hiero's fear or distrust of Simonides originates in his attitude towards wise men, and would exist regardless of the topic of their conversation. But if there were any one topic which could aggravate Hiero's suspicion of Simonides, it is that topic which the wise man in fact proposed—a topic relating to the object with regard to which the tyrants fear the wise. In addition, Simonides explicitly says that all men regard tyrants with a mixture of admiration and envy, or that they are jealous of tyrants, and Hiero

understands the bearing of this statement sufficiently to apply it to
Simonides by speaking of Simonides himself being jealous of
tyrants.[36] Hiero does not possess that true understanding of the
nature of wisdom which alone could protect him from being
suspicious of Simonides' question about the relative desirability of
tyrannical and private life. Lacking such understanding, Hiero
cannot be certain that the question might not serve the very practical purpose of eliciting some first-hand information from the tyrant
about a condition of which the poet is jealous or to which he is
aspiring for himself or someone else. His fear or distrust of Simonides will be a fear or distrust strengthened and rendered definite
by Simonides' apparently believing that the tyrannical life is more
desirable than private life. Simonides' apparently frank confession
of his preference will seem to Hiero to supply him with an opportunity of getting rid of his uneasiness. His whole answer will serve
the very practical purpose of dissuading Simonides from looking at
tyrants with a mixture of admiration and envy.

By playing upon this intention of Hiero,[37] Simonides compels
him to use the strongest possible language against tyranny and thus
finally to declare his bankruptcy, therewith handing over the
leadership in the conversation to Simonides. Simonides' intention
to dishearten Hiero and Hiero's intention to dissuade Simonides
from admiring or envying tyrants produce by their co-operation the
result primarily intended by Simonides, viz., a situation in which
Hiero has no choice but to listen to Simonides' advice.

In order to provoke Hiero's passionate reaction, Simonides has
to overstate the case for tyranny. When reading all his statements
by themselves, one is struck by the fact that there are indeed some
passages in which he, more or less compelled by Hiero's arguments,
grants that tyranny has its drawbacks, whereas one finds more
passages in which he spontaneously and strongly asserts its advantages. The statements of Simonides on tyranny would justify
Hiero in thinking that Simonides is envious of tyrants. Yet the
ironical character of Simonides' praise of tyranny as such (as distinguished from his praise of beneficent tyranny in the second part
of the *Hiero*) can hardly escape the notice of any reader. For instance, when he asserts that tyrants derive greater pleasure from

sounds than private men because they constantly hear the most pleasant kind of sound, viz., praise, he is not ignorant of the fact that the praise bestowed upon tyrants by their entourage is not genuine praise.[38] On the other hand, Hiero is interested in overstating the case against tyranny. This point requires some discussion since the explicit indictment of tyranny in the *Hiero* is entrusted exclusively to Hiero, and therefore the understanding of the tendency of the *Hiero* as a whole depends decisively on the correct appreciation of Hiero's utterances on the subject.

It is certainly inadmissible to take for granted that Hiero simply voices Xenophon's considered judgment on tyranny: Hiero is not Xenophon. Besides, there is some specific evidence which goes to show that Hiero's indictment of tyranny is, according to Xenophon's view, exaggerated. Hiero asserts that *"the* cities magnificently honor the tyrannicide"; Xenophon, however, tells us that those murderers of Jason who survived were honored "in *most* of the Greek cities" to which they came.[39] Hiero asserts that the tyrants "know well that *all* their subjects are their enemies"; Xenophon, however, tells us that the subjects of the tyrant Euphron considered him their benefactor and revered him highly.[40] Hiero describes the tyrant as deprived of all pleasures of gay companionship; Xenophon, however, describes the tyrant Astyages as securely enjoying those pleasures to the full.[41] Yet Hiero may have said more against tyranny than Xenophon would grant; he may still have said exactly what he himself thought about the subject on the basis of his bitter experiences. Now, no reader however careful of the speeches of Hiero can possibly know anything of the expression of Hiero's face, of his gestures, and of the inflections of his voice. He is then not in the best position to detect which words of Hiero's rang true and which rang false. It is one of the many advantages of a dialogue one character of which is a wise man, that it puts at the disposal of the reader the wise man's discriminating observations concerning the different degree of reliability of the various utterances which flow with an equal ease, but not necessarily with an equal degree of conviction, from his companion's mouth. When reading the *Hiero* cursorily, one is bound to feel that Hiero is worried particularly by the tyrant's lack of friendship, confidence, patriotism, and true honor as well as by the constant danger of assassination. Yet Xenophon's Simonides, who is our sole authority for the adequate interpretation of the speeches of Xenophon's Hiero, was definitely not under the impression that Hiero's greatest sorrow was caused by the lack of the noble things mentioned, or by those agonies of perpetual and limitless fear which he describes in so edifying a manner. He has not the slightest doubt that Hiero has blamed tyranny most of all with a view to the fact that the tyrant is deprived of the sweetest pleasures of homosexual love, i.e., of pleasures which Simonides himself declares to be of minor importance.[42] Simonides is then not greatly impressed by Hiero's indictment of tyranny. That indictment, however touching or eloquent, has therefore to be read with a great deal of reasonable distrust.

When proving that private men derive greater pleasure from victory than tyrants, Hiero compares the victory of the citizens over their foreign enemies with the victory of the tyrant over his subjects: the citizens consider their victory something noble, and they are proud of it and boast of it, whereas the tyrant cannot be proud of his victory, or boast of it, or consider it noble.[43] Hiero fails to mention, not only the victory of a party in a civil war, but above all the victory of the citizens governed or led by their tyrannical ruler over their foreign enemies: he forgets his own victory in the battle of Cumae. He fails to consider the obvious possibility that a tyrant, who takes the chief responsibility for the outcome of a war, might be more gratified by victory than might the ordinary citizen; for it was the prudent counsel and efficient leadership of the tyrant that brought about the happy issue, while the ordinary citizen never can have had more than a small share in the deliberations concerning the war. Hiero fails to consider that this great pleasure might fully compensate the tyrant for the lack of many lesser pleasures.

We may speak of a twofold meaning of the indictment of tyranny which forms the first and by far the largest part of the *Hiero*. According to its obvious meaning, it amounts to the strongest possible indictment of tyranny: the greatest possible authority on the subject, a tyrant who as such speaks from experience, shows that tyranny is bad even from the point of view of tyrants, even

from the point of view of the pleasures of the tyrant.[44] This meaning is obvious; one merely has to read the first part of the *Hiero,*
which consists chiefly of speeches of Hiero to this effect, in order
to grasp it. A less obvious meaning of the first part of the *Hiero*
comes into sight as soon as one considers its conversational setting—
the fact that the distrustful tyrant is speaking *pro domo*—and, going
one step further in the same direction, when one considers the
facts recorded in Xenophon's historical work (the *Hellenica*).
These considerations lead one to a more qualified indictment of
tyranny, or to a more truthful account of tyranny, or to the wise
view of tyranny. This means that in order to grasp Xenophon's
view of tyranny as distinguished from Hiero's utterances about
tyranny, one has to consider Hiero's "speeches" in the light of the
more trustworthy "deeds" or "actions" or "facts," [45] and in particular that most important of "facts," the conversational setting of
the *Hiero.* To the two meanings correspond then two types of reading, and ultimately two types of men. It was with a view to this difference between types of men and a corresponding difference between types of speaking that Socrates liked to quote the verses from
the *Iliad* in which Odysseus is described as using different language when speaking to outstanding men on the one hand, and
when speaking to the common people on the other; [46] and that
he distinguished the superficial understanding of Homer on the
part of the rhapsodes from that understanding which grasps the
poet's "insinuations." [47] The superficial understanding is not simply
wrong, since it grasps the obvious meaning which is as much intended by the author as is the deeper meaning. To describe in one
sentence the art employed by Xenophon in the first part of the
Hiero, we may say that by choosing a conversational setting in
which the strongest possible indictment of tyranny becomes necessary, he intimates the limited validity of that indictment.[48]

b. The action of the dialogue

No genuine communication could develop if Hiero were animated exclusively by distrust of Simonides, or if Simonides did not
succeed in gaining the tyrant's confidence to some extent. At the
beginning of the conversation he reassures Hiero by declaring his

willingness to learn from Hiero, i.e., to trust him in what he is going
to say about the relative desirability of tyrannical and private life.
The first section of the dialogue (ch. 1) is characterized by the
interplay of Simonides' intention to reassure Hiero with his intention to dishearten him. That interplay ceases as soon as Hiero is
completely committed to the continuance of the conversation. From
that moment Simonides limits himself to provoking Hiero to express
his unqualified indictment of tyranny.

Hiero, perhaps offended by Simonides' inevitable reference to
his pre-tyrannical past and at the same time desirous to know more
about Simonides' intentions and his preferences, emphasizes how
remote he considers that past by asking Simonides to remind him
of the pleasures and pains of private men: he pretends to have
forgotten them.[1] In this context he mentions the fact that Simonides is "at present still a private man." Simonides seems to accept
the challenge for a moment. At any rate, he makes to begin with a
distinction between himself and private men ("I seem to have
observed that private men enjoy . . ."); but he soon drops that
odious distinction by identifying himself unreservedly with the
private men ("We seem to enjoy . . .").[2] In complying with Hiero's
request, Simonides enumerates various groups of pleasurable and
painful things. The enumeration is in a sense complete: it covers
the pleasures and pains of the body, those of the soul, and those
common to body and soul. Otherwise, it is most surprising. While
it is unnecessarily detailed as regards the pleasures and pains of the
body, it does not give any details whatsoever as regards the other
kinds of pleasure and pain mentioned. It is reasonable to assume
that the selection is made, at least partly, *ad hominem,* or that it is
meant to prepare a discussion which serves a specific practical purpose. Simonides enumerates seven groups of things which are sometimes pleasant and sometimes painful for private men, and one
which is always pleasant for them: that which is always pleasant
for them is sleep—which the tyrant, haunted by fears of all kinds,
must strive to avoid.[3] This example seems to show that the purpose
of Simonides' enumeration is to remind the tyrant of the pleasures
of which he is supposed to be deprived, and thus to induce him to
make clear to himself the misery of tyrannical life. It is for this

reason, one might surmise to begin with, that the enumeration puts the emphasis on the pleasures of the body,[4] i.e., on those pleasures the enjoyment of which is not characteristic of actual or potential tyrants. However, if Simonides' chief intention had been to remind Hiero of the pleasures of which he is actually or supposedly deprived, he would not have dropped the topic "sleep" in the discussion which immediately follows (in ch. 1). Furthermore, Simonides' initial enumeration fails to have any depressing effect on Hiero. It seems therefore preferable to say that his emphasizing the pleasures of the body in the initial enumeration is chiefly due to his intention to reassure Hiero. Emphasizing these pleasures, he creates the impression that he is himself chiefly interested in them. But men chiefly interested in bodily pleasures are not likely to aspire to any ruling position.[5]

Hiero is satisfied with Simonides' enumeration. He gives Simonides to understand that it exhausts the types of pleasure and pain experienced by tyrants as well as by private men. Simonides strikes the first obvious note of dissonance by asserting that the life of a tyrant contains many more pleasures of all kinds and many fewer pains of all kinds than private life. Hiero's immediate answer is still restrained. He does not assert that tyrannical life is inferior to private life as such; he merely says that tyrannical life is inferior to the life of private men of moderate means.[6] He admits by implication that the condition of tyrants is preferable to that of poor men. Yet poverty and wealth are to be measured, not by number, but with a view to use, or to need.[7] At least from this point of view, Simonides may be poor and hence justified in being jealous of tyrants. At any rate, he now reveals that he looks at tyrants with a mixture of admiration and envy and that he might belong to the "many who are reputed to be most able men" who desire to be tyrants. The tension increases. Hiero strengthens his reply, which is more emphatic than any previous utterance of his, by an oath, and he expresses his intention to teach Simonides the truth about the relative desirability of tyrannical and private life.[8] Speaking as a teacher, he embarks upon a discussion of the various kinds of bodily pleasure which keeps in the main to the order followed by Simonides in his initial enumeration.[9] Hiero now tries to prove the thesis that tyrannical life is inferior, not merely to a specific private life, but to private life as such.[10]

The discussion of bodily pleasures (1.10-38) reveals the preferences of the two interlocutors in an indirect way.[11] According to Hiero, the inferiority of tyranny shows itself most clearly with regard to the pleasures of sex, and especially of homosexuality.[12] The only proper name occurring in the *Hiero* (apart from those of Simonides, Hiero, Zeus, and the Greeks), i.e., the only concrete reference to Hiero's life, as well as Hiero's second emphatic oath (which is his last emphatic oath), occurs in the passage dealing with homosexual love.[13] Simonides is particularly vocal regarding the pleasures of hearing, i.e., the pleasures of hearing praise, and, above all, regarding the pleasures of food. His most emphatic assertion, occurring in the discussion of bodily pleasures, concerns food.[14] Two of his five "by Zeus" occur in the passage dealing with food.[15] That passage is the only part of the *Hiero* where the conversation takes on the character of a lively discussion, and in fact of a Socratic elenchus (with Hiero in the role of Socrates): Hiero is compelled, point by point, to refute Simonides' assertion that tyrants derive greater pleasure from food than private men.[16] Only in reading the discussion concerning food does one get the impression that Hiero has to overcome a serious resistance on the part of Simonides: four times he appeals from Simonides' assertion to Simonides' experience, observation, or knowledge. How much Hiero is aware of this state of things is shown by the fact that after Simonides had already abandoned the subject, Hiero once more returns to it in order to leave no doubt whatsoever in Simonides' mind as to the inferiority of tyrannical life in the matter of the pleasures of the table: he does not rest until Simonides has granted that, as regards these pleasures, tyrants are worse off than private men.[17] As an explanation we suggest that Simonides wants to reassure Hiero by presenting himself as a man chiefly interested in food, or in "good living" in general, or by ironically overstating his actual liking for "good living."[18]

At the end of the discussion of the bodily pleasures, we seem to have reached the end of the whole conversation. Simonides had originally enumerated eight groups of pleasurable or painful things: 1) sights, 2) sounds, 3) odors, 4) food and drink, 5) sex, 6) objects perceived by the whole body, 7) good and bad things, and 8) sleep. After four of them (sights, sounds, food and drink, odors) have been discussed, he says that the pleasures of sex seem to be the only motive which excites in tyrants the desire for tyrannical rule.[19] By implication, he thus dismisses as irrelevant three of the four groups of pleasant or painful things which had not thereto been discussed (objects perceived by the whole body, good and bad things, sleep). Hence, he narrows down the whole question of the relative desirability of tyrannical and private life to the question, Do tyrants or private men enjoy to a higher degree the pleasures of sex? So doing, he completely reassures Hiero: he practically capitulates. For of nothing is Hiero more convinced than of this, that precisely as regards the pleasures of sex, tyrants are most evidently worse off than private men. He is so much convinced of the truth of his thesis and of the decisive character of the argument by which he upholds it, that he can speak later on of his having "demonstrated" to Simonides the true character of a tyrant's amatory pleasures.[20] At the end of the discussion of sex, i.e., at the end of the discussion of the bodily pleasures, Hiero has proved to Simonides what the latter had admitted to be the only point which still needed proof if Hiero's general thesis were to be established securely. On the level of the surface argument the discussion has reached its end. The discussion would have reached its end as well, if Simonides had no other intention than to find out what Hiero's greatest worries are, or to remind him of the pleasures from the lack of which he suffers most, or to give him an opportunity of speaking freely of what disturbs him most. All these aims have been reached at the end of the discussion of sex: Hiero is concerned most of all with the tyrant's lack of the sweetest pleasures of homosexual love,[21] and the later discussion is devoted to entirely different subjects. On the other hand, the continuation of the conversation is evidently necessary if Simonides' intention is to defeat Hiero by playing upon the tyrant's fear of the wise.

The first round ends, so it seems, with a complete victory for Hiero. He has proved his thesis without saying too much against tyranny and therewith against himself. Now the struggle begins

in earnest. In the preceding part of the conversation, Simonides'
expressions of jealousy of the tyrants had been mitigated, if not
altogether retracted, by his emphasis on the pleasures of the body.
Now he declares in glaring contrast to all that has gone before,
and in particular to what he has said about the unique significance
of the pleasures of sex, that the whole preceding discussion is
irrelevant, because it dealt only with what he believes to be very
minor matters: many of those who are reputed to be (real) men
(ἄνδρες)[22] just despise the bodily pleasures; they aspire to greater
things, namely, to power and wealth; it is in relation to wealth and
power that tyrannical life is manifestly superior to private life. In
the preceding part of the conversation, Simonides had tacitly identified himself with the vulgar; now he tacitly makes a distinction
between himself and the vulgar. But the non-vulgar type to which
he tacitly claims to belong is not the type of the "gentleman" but
of the "real man." [23] While elaborating the thesis that tyrannical
life brings greater wealth and power than private life, he supple-
ments his initial enumeration of pleasurable and painful things
(in which the "good or bad" things have almost disappeared
amidst the throng of objects of bodily pleasure) by an enumeration of the elements of power and wealth. In doing this, he seems
to imply that power and wealth are unambiguously "good" and
in fact the only things that matter.[24] Since Simonides knows that
Hiero considers him a real man, and since he declares explicitly that
he himself considers the bodily pleasures as of very minor importance, Simonides thus intimates [25] an unequivocal taste for tyranny.
In enumerating the various elements of power and wealth, he
reveals his taste more specifically, and more subtly, by what he
mentions and by what he fails to mention.[26]

From this moment the conversation changes its character in
a surprising manner. Whereas Simonides had been fairly vocal
during the rather short discussion of the bodily pleasures (his contribution consisting of about 218 words out of 1058), he is almost
completely silent during the much more extensive discussion of
the good or bad things (his contribution consisting of 28 words
out of about 2000). Besides, the discussion of the bodily pleasures
had kept, in the main, to the items and the sequence suggested in

Simonides' initial enumeration, and this had been due largely to Simonides' almost continuous interference with Hiero's exposition. But now, in the discussion of the good or bad things, Hiero deviates considerably, not to say completely, from Simonides' enumeration of these things and their sequence by introducing topics which had barely been hinted at by Simonides.[27] The purpose of Hiero's procedure is evident. In the first place, he can refute only with difficulty the cautious assertion to which the wise Simonides had limited himself,[28] that the tyrant possesses greater power and wealth than private men. Above all, he is very anxious to push "wealth" into the background in favor of the other good things because wealth is so highly desired by "real men" of the type of Simonides as well as by the actual tyrant himself.[29] The topics not mentioned by Simonides but introduced by Hiero are: peace and war, friendship,[30] confidence, fatherland, good men, city and citizens, fear and protection. Simonides' declaration asserting the superiority of tyrants as regards power and wealth provokes Hiero to an eloquent indictment of tyranny which surpasses in scope everything said in the first section: the tyrant is cut off from such good things as peace, the pleasant aspects of war, friendship, confidence, fatherland, and the company of good men; he is hated and conspired against by his nearest relatives and friends; he cannot enjoy the greatness of his own fatherland; he lives in perpetual fear for his life; he is compelled to commit grave crimes against gods and men; those who kill him, far from being punished, are greatly honored. Simonides has succeeded in increasing Hiero's tenseness far beyond the limits which it had reached during the discussion of the bodily pleasures. This shows itself particularly in those passages where the tyrant speaks of subjects already mentioned in the first section.[31] And this increase of tension is due, not only to the declaration with which the poet had opened the second round, but, above all, to the ambiguous silence with which he listens to Hiero's tirade. Is he overawed by Hiero's indictment of tyranny? Does he doubt Hiero's sincerity? Or is he just bored by Hiero's speech because his chief concern is with "food," with the pleasures of the body, the discussion of which had interested him sufficiently to make him talk? Hiero cannot know.

The meaning of Simonides' silence is partly revealed by its immediate consequence. It leads to the consequence that the topics introduced by Hiero are hardly as much as mentioned, and certainly not discussed by Simonides in the first two sections of the dialogue. His silence thus brings out in full relief the contrast between the topics introduced in the first two sections by Hiero on the one hand, and by Simonides on the other. Simonides introduces the pleasures of the body as well as wealth and power; Hiero introduces the loftier things. Simonides, who has to convince Hiero of his competence to give sound advice to tyrants, must guard by all means against appearing in Hiero's eyes as a poet: he limits himself to speaking about the more pedestrian things.[32] Hiero, who tries to dissuade Simonides from being jealous of tyrants, or from aspiring to tyranny, has to appeal from Simonides' craving for low things to his more noble aspirations. The lesson which Xenophon ironically conveys by this element of the conversational setting seems to be this: a teacher of tyrants has to appear as a hardboiled man; it does not do any harm if he makes his pupil suspect that he cannot be impressed by considerations of a more noble character.

The poet interrupts his silence only once. The circumstances of that interruption call for some attention. Hiero had given Simonides more than one opportunity to say something, especially by addressing him by name.[33] This applies especially to his discussion of friendship. Therein one can almost see Hiero urging him towards at least some visible reaction.[34] After all his efforts to make Simonides talk have failed, he turns to what he considers the characteristic pleasures of private men: drink, song, and sleep, which he, having become a tyrant, cannot enjoy any longer because he is perpetually harassed by fear, the spoiler of all pleasures.[35] Simonides remains silent. Hiero makes a last attempt, this one more successful. Reminding himself of the fact that Simonides had been most vocal while food was being discussed, he replaces "strong drink and sleep" by "food and sleep."[36] Referring to the poet's possible experience of fear in battle, he asserts that tyrants can enjoy food and sleep as little as, or less than, soldiers who have the enemy's phalanx close in front of them. Simonides replies that his military experience proves to him the possibility of combining "living dangerously" with a healthy appetite and a sound sleep.[37] Saying this, he tacitly denies more strongly than by his statement at the beginning of the second section the reassuring implications of his previous emphasis on the pleasures of the body.[38]

We must now step back and look again at the picture as a whole. Taken as a whole, the second section consists of Hiero's sweeping indictment of tyranny, to which Simonides listens in silence. The meaning of this silence is finally revealed by what happens in the third section (ch. 7). The third section, the shortest section of the *Hiero,* contains, or immediately prepares for, the peripeteia. It culminates in Hiero's declaration that the tyrant can hardly do better than to hang himself. By making this declaration, Hiero abdicates the leadership in the conversation in favor of Simonides who keeps it throughout the fourth and last section (ch. 8-11).[39] We contend that this crucial event—Hiero's breakdown or the change from Hiero's leadership to Simonides' leadership—is consciously and decisively prepared by Simonides' remaining silent in the second section.

The third section opens again with a surprising move of Simonides.[40] He grants to Hiero that tyranny is as toilsome and as dangerous as the latter had asserted; yet, he says, those toils and dangers are reasonably borne because they lead to the pleasure deriving from honors, and no other human pleasure comes nearer to divinity than this kind of pleasure: tyrants are honored more than any other men. In the parallel at the beginning of the second section Simonides had spoken only of what *"many* of those who are *reputed* to be (real) men" desire, and had merely implied that what they desire is power and wealth. Now he openly declares that the desire for honor is characteristic of real men as such, i.e., as distinguished from ordinary "human beings."[41] There seems to be no longer any doubt that Simonides, who is admittedly a real man, longs for tyrannical power.

Hiero's immediate reply reveals that he is more alarmed than ever before. He had mentioned before the facts that the tyrant is in perpetual danger of being assassinated and that tyrants com-

mit acts of injustice. But never before had he mentioned these two
facts within one and the same sentence. Still less had he explicitly
established a connection between them. Only now, while trying to
prove that the tyrant does not derive any pleasure from the honors
shown to him, does he declare that the tyrant spends night and
day like one condemned by all men to die for his injustice.[42] One
might think for a moment that this increase in the vehemence of
Hiero's indictment of tyranny is due to the subject matter so unex-
pectedly introduced by Simonides: Hiero might seem to suffer
most of all from the fact that the tyrant is deprived of genuine
honor. But if this is the case, why does he not protest against
Simonides' later remark that Hiero had depreciated tyranny most
because it frustrated the tyrant's homosexual desires? Why did
he not bring up the subject of "honor" himself instead of waiting
until Simonides did it? Why did he not find fault with Simonides'
misleading initial enumeration of pleasures? Last but not least,
why did the earlier discussion of a similar subject—praise [43]—fail
to make any noticeable impression on his mood? It is not so much
the intrinsic significance of Simonides' statement on honor as its
conversational significance, which accounts for its conspicuous and
indeed decisive effect.

At the beginning of his statement on honor, Simonides alludes
to Hiero's description of the toils and dangers which attend the life
of a tyrant. But Hiero had described not merely those toils and
dangers, but also the moral depravity to which the tyrant is condemned: he is compelled to live "by contriving something bad
and base"; he is compelled to commit the crime of robbing temples
and men; he cannot be a true patriot; he desires to enslave his
fellow-citizens; only the consideration that a tyrant must have
living subjects who walk around, seems to prevent him from killing
or imprisoning all his subjects. After Hiero has finished his long
speech, Simonides declares that in spite of everything that the
tyrant has said, tyranny is highly desirable because it leads to
supreme honor. As regards the toils and dangers pointed out by
Hiero, Simonides pauses to allude to them; as regards the moral
flaws deplored by Hiero, he simply ignores them. That is to say,
the poet is not at all impressed by the immorality, or the injustice,

characteristic of the tyrannical life; certainly its inevitable immorality would not prevent him for a moment from aspiring to
tyranny for the sake of honor. No wonder then that Hiero collapses
shortly afterwards: what overwhelms him is not Simonides' statement on honor itself, but the poet's making it in this particular
context. Because it is made in that context, and merely because
it is made in that context, does it make Hiero realize to what
lengths a man of Simonides' exceptional "wisdom" could go in
"contriving something" and in particular in "contriving something
bad and base." It is by thus silently, i.e., most astutely, revealing a
complete lack of scruple that the poet both overwhelms Hiero and
convinces him of his competence to give sound advice to a tyrant.[44]

The lesson which Xenophon conveys by making Simonides
listen silently to Hiero's long speech, as well as by his answer to
that speech, can now be stated as follows. Even a perfectly just
man who wants to give advice to a tyrant has to present himself to
his pupil as an utterly unscrupulous man. The greatest man who
ever imitated the *Hiero* was Machiavelli. I should not be sur-
prised if a sufficiently attentive study of Machiavelli's work would
lead to the conclusion that it is precisely Machiavelli's perfect
understanding of Xenophon's chief pedagogic lesson which
accounts for the most shocking sentences occurring in the *Prince*.
But if Machiavelli understood Xenophon's lesson, he certainly did
not apply it in the spirit of its originator. For, according to Xenophon, the teacher of tyrants has to appear as an utterly unscrupulous man, not by protesting that he does not fear hell nor devil,
nor by expressing immoral principles, but by simply failing to take
notice of the moral principles. He has to reveal his alleged or real
freedom from morality, not by speech, but by silence. For by doing
so—by disregarding morality "by deed" rather than by attacking
it "by speech"—he reveals at the same time his understanding of
political things. Xenophon, or his Simonides, is more "politic"
than Machiavelli; he refuses to separate "moderation" (prudence)
from "wisdom" (insight).

By replying to Hiero's long speech in the manner described,
Simonides compels him to use still stronger language against
tyranny than he had done before. Now Hiero declares that a

tyrant, as distinguished from a man who is a benefactor of his fellows and therefore genuinely honored, lives like one condemned by all men to die for his injustice. Arrived at this point, Simonides could have replied in the most natural manner that, this being the case, the tyrant ought to rule as beneficently as possible. He could have begun at once to teach Hiero how to rule well as a tyrant. But he apparently felt that he needed some further information for sizing Hiero up, or that Hiero needed a further shock before he would be prepared to listen. Therefore he asks Hiero why, if tyranny is really such a great evil for the tyrant, neither he nor any other tyrant ever yet gave up his position voluntarily. Hiero answers that no tyrant can abdicate because he cannot make amends for the robbing, imprisoning, and killing of his subjects; (just as it does not profit him to live as a tyrant, it does not profit him to live again as a private man) ; if it profits any man (to cease living), to hang himself, it profits the tyrant most of all.[45] This answer puts the finishing touch to the preparation for Simonides' instruction. Simonides' final attack had amounted to a veiled suggestion addressed to the tyrant to return to private life. That suggestion is the necessary conclusion which a reasonable man would draw from Hiero's comparison between tyrannical and private life. Hiero defends himself against that suggestion by revealing what might seem to be some rudimentary sense of justice : he cannot return to private life because he cannot make amends for the many acts of injustice which he has committed. This defense is manifestly hypocritical : if tyranny is what he has asserted it to be, he prefers heaping new crimes on the untold number of crimes which he has already committed rather than stop his criminal career and suffer the consequences of his former misdeeds. His real motive for not abdicating seems then to be fear of punishment. But could he not escape punishment by simply fleeing? This is indeed the crucial implication of Hiero's last word against tyranny : as if there never had been a tyrant who, after having been expelled from his city, lived quietly thereafter in exile, and although he himself had said on a former occasion [46] that while making a journey abroad, the tyrant might easily be deposed, Hiero refuses to consider the possibility of escape from his city. He thus reveals himself as a man who is unable to live as a stranger.[47] It is this citizen spirit of his—the fact that he cannot help being absolutely attached to his city—to which the wandering poet silently appeals when teaching him how to be a good ruler.

Hiero has finally been rendered incapable of any further move. He has been reduced to a condition in which he has to fetter himself by a sincere or insincere assertion, or in which he has to use the language of a man who is despondent. He uses entirely different language in the two fairly brief utterances which he makes in the fourth or last section. Whereas his indictment of tyranny in the first part of the *Hiero* had presented the tyrant as the companion of the unjust and had culminated in the description of the tyrant as injustice incarnate, he describes him in the last part of the dialogue—i.e., a few minutes later—as a man who punishes the unjust,[48] as a defender of justice. This quick change of language, or of attitude, is most astonishing. As we have seen, the vehemence of Hiero's indictment had been increasing from section to section because Simonides had not been deterred from praising tyranny by the shortcomings of tyranny pointed out by Hiero. Now, Hiero had spoken against tyranny in the third section more violently than ever before, and in the fourth section Simonides continues praising tyranny.[49] Hence one should expect that Hiero will continue still increasing the vehemence of his indictment of tyranny. Yet he takes the opposite course. What has happened? Why does Simonides' praise of tyranny in the fourth section, and especially in the early part of that section (8. 1-7), fail to arouse Hiero's violent reaction? We suggest the following answer: Simonides' praise of tyranny in the fourth section—as distinguished from his praise of tyranny in the preceding sections—is not considered by Hiero an expression of the poet's jealousy of tyrants. More precisely, Simonides' immediate reaction to Hiero's statement that a tyrant can hardly do better than to hang himself, or the use which Simonides makes of his newly acquired leadership, convinces Hiero that the poet is not concerned with "contriving something" of an undesirable character. The action by which Simonides breaks down the walls of Hiero's distrust, is the peripeteia of the dialogue.

The difficult position into which Hiero has been forced is not without its advantages. Hiero had been on the defensive because he did not know what Simonides might be contriving. By his defeat, by his declaration of bankruptcy, he succeeds in stopping Simonides to the extent that he forces him to show his hand. He presents himself as a man who knows that neither of the two ways of life—the tyrannical and the private life—profits him, but who does not know whether it would profit him to cease living by hanging himself (" *if* it profits any man . . .").[50] Simonides could have taken up in a fairly natural manner the question implicitly raised by Hiero as to whether suicide is an advisable course of action, and in particular whether there are not other forms of death preferable to, or easier than, hanging.[51] In other words, the poet could conceivably have tried to persuade the tyrant to commit suicide, or to commit suicide in the easiest manner. To exaggerate grossly for purposes of clarification : the victory of the wise man over the tyrant, achieved solely by means of speech prudently interspersed with silence, is so complete that the wise man could kill the tyrant without lifting a finger, employing only speech, only persuasion. But he does nothing of the kind : he who has the power of persuasion, he who can do what he likes with any interlocutor, prefers to make use of the obedience of a living man rather than to kill him.[52] After having made Hiero realize fully that a wise man has the power of going to any length in contriving anything, Simonides gives him to understand that the wise man would not make use of this power. Simonides' refraining from acting like a man who wants to do away with a tyrant, or to deprive him of his power, is the decisive reason for the change in Hiero's attitude.

But silence is not enough : Simonides has to say something. What he says is determined by his intention to advise Hiero, and by the impossibility of advising a man who is despondent. It is immaterial in this respect that Hiero's complaints about his situation are of questionable sincerity; for Simonides is not in a position openly to question their sincerity. He has then to comfort Hiero while advising him or prior to advising him. Accordingly, his teaching of the tyrannical art is presented in the following form : Tyranny is most desirable ("comfort") if you will only do such and such things ("advice"). The comfort element of Simonides' teaching—

the praise of (beneficent) tyranny—is due to the conversational situation and cannot be presumed to be an integral part of Xenophon's teaching concerning tyranny until it has been proved to be so. On the other hand, Simonides' advice can be presumed from the outset to be identical with Xenophon's suggestions about the improvement of tyrannical rule as a radically faulty political order.

It would not have been impossible for Simonides to refute Hiero by showing that the latter's account of tyranny is exaggerated, i.e., by discussing Hiero's indictment of tyranny point by point. But such a detailed discussion would merely have led to the conclusion that tyranny is not quite as bad as Hiero had asserted. That dreary result would not have sufficed for restoring Hiero's courage or for counteracting the crushing effect of his final verdict on tyranny. Or, to disregard for one moment the conversational setting, an exact examination of Hiero's arguments would have destroyed completely the edifying effect of the indictment of tyranny in the first part of the *Hiero*. Xenophon had then to burden his Simonides with the task of drawing a picture of tyranny which would be at least as bright as the one drawn by Hiero had been dark. The abundant use of the *modus potentialis* in Simonides' speech as well as the silence of the *Hiero* and indeed of the whole *Corpus Xenophonteum* about happy tyrants who actually existed anywhere in Greece, make it certain that Simonides' praise of tyranny in the second part of the *Hiero* was considered by Xenophon even more rhetorical than Hiero's indictment of tyranny in the first part.

Hiero had tried to show that tyrannical life is inferior to private life from the point of view of pleasure. In the existing situation, Simonides cannot appeal directly from the pleasant to the noble, for Hiero had just declared in the most emphatic manner that, as a matter of fact, a tyrant is a man who has committed an untold number of crimes. Simonides is therefore compelled to show (what in the first part he had hardly more than asserted) that tyrannical life is superior to private life from the point of view of pleasure. Being compelled to accept the tyrant's end, he must show that Hiero used the wrong means. In other words, he must trace Hiero's being out of heart with tyranny, not to a wrong intention, but to an error of judgment, to an erroneous belief.[53]

Simonides discovers the specific error which he ascribes to Hiero by reflecting on the latter's reply to the poet's statement concerning honor. Hiero had compared the honors enjoyed by tyrants with their sexual pleasures: just as services rendered by those who do not love in turn, or who act under compulsion, are no favors, services rendered by those who fear, are no honors. The *tertium comparationis* between the pleasures of sex and those of honor is that both must be granted by people who are prompted by love (φιλία) and not by fear. Now Hiero is worried most by his being deprived of the genuine pleasures of sex. But Simonides might offend him by emphasizing this fact and thus asserting that Hiero is more concerned with sex than with honor and hence perhaps not a "real man." He elegantly avoids this embarrassment by escaping into something more general, viz., into that which is common to "honor" and "sex." [54] For whether Hiero is chiefly concerned with the one or the other, he is in both cases in need of love (φιλία). And in both cases his misery is due to his belief that being a tyrant and being loved are mutually exclusive.[55] This is then the diagnosis of Hiero's illness from which Simonides starts: Hiero is out of heart with tyranny because, desiring to be loved by human beings, he believes that tyrannical rule prevents him from being so loved.[56] Simonides does not limit himself to rejecting this belief. He asserts that tyrants are more likely to gain affection than private men. For whatever might have to be said against tyranny, the tyrant is certainly a ruler, hence a man of high standing among his fellows, and "we" naturally admire men of high social standing. Above all, the prestige attending ruling positions adds an unbought grace to any act of kindness performed by rulers in general and hence by tyrants in particular.[57] It is by means of this assertion that Simonides surreptitiously suggests his cure for Hiero's illness, a cure discovered, just as the illness itself was, by reflecting on Hiero's comparison of "honor" and "sex." Hiero had granted as a matter of course that in order to receive favors, to be loved in return, one must first love: the misery of the tyrant consists in the very fact that he loves and is not loved in turn.[58] Simonides tacitly applies what Hiero had granted as regards sexual love, to love in general: he who wants to be loved, must love first; he who wants to be loved by his subjects in order to be genuinely honored by them, must love them first; to gain favors, he must first show favors. He does not state this lesson in so many words, but he transmits it implicitly by comparing the effects of a tyrant's acts of kindness with the effects of a private man's acts of kindness. He thus shifts the emphasis almost insensibly from the pleasant feelings primarily desired to the noble or praiseworthy actions which directly or indirectly bring about those pleasant feelings. He tacitly advises the tyrant to think, not of his own pleasures, but of the pleasures of others; not of his being served and receiving gifts, but of his doing services and making gifts.[59] That is to say, he tacitly gives the tyrant exactly the same advice which Socrates explicitly gives his companions, nay, which Virtue herself explicitly gives to Heracles.[60]

Simonides' virtuous advice does not spoil the effect of his previous indifference to moral principles because the virtuous character of his advice is sufficiently qualified by the context in which it is given. Socrates and Virtue shout their advice from the housetops to men who are of normal decency, and even potential paragons of virtue. Simonides, on the other hand, suggests substantially the same advice in the most subdued language to a tyrant who has just confessed having committed an untold number of crimes. It is true, Simonides' language becomes considerably less restrained towards the end of the conversation. But it is also true that throughout the conversation he presents the pleasant effects of a tyrant's kind actions as wholly independent of the manner in which the tyrant had come to power and of any of his previous misdeeds. Simonides' alleged or real freedom from scruple is preserved in, and operates in, his very recommendation of virtue.[61]

Hiero answers "straightway," "at once." This is the only occasion on which either of the two interlocutors says something "straightway." [62] It is Simonides' reaction to Hiero's statement that the tyrant can hardly do better than to hang himself, which induces the tyrant to answer "at once," i.e., to proceed without that slowness, or circumspection, which characterizes all other utterances of the two men. Dropping his habitual reserve, Hiero gives a sincere, not exaggerated account of the difficulties confronting the tyrant. He no longer denies that tyrants have greater power than private men to do things by means of which men gain affection; he merely denies that they are for this reason more likely to be loved than private men, because they are also compelled to do very many things by which men incur hatred. Thus, e.g., they have to exact money and to punish the unjust; and, above all, they are in need of mercenaries.[63] Simonides does not say that one should not take care of all these matters.[64] But, he believes, there are ways of taking care of things which lead to hatred and other ways which lead to gratification: a ruler should himself do the gratifying things (such as the awarding of prizes) while entrusting to others the hateful things (such as the inflicting of punishment). The implication of this advice as well as of all other advice given to Hiero by Simonides is, of course, that Hiero needs such advice, or that he is actually doing the opposite of what Simonides is advising him to do, i.e., that he is at present a most imperfect ruler. Imitating in his speech by anticipation the hoped-for behavior of his pupil Hiero, or rather giving him by his own action an example of the behavior proper to a tyrant, Simonides soon drops all explicit mention of the hateful things inseparable from tyranny, if not from government as such, while he praises the enormous usefulness of offering prizes: the hateful aspects of tyranny are not indeed annihilated, but banished from sight.[65] Simonides' praise of beneficent tyranny thus serves the purpose not merely of comforting Hiero (who is certainly much less in need of comfort than his utterances might induce the unwary reader to believe), but above all of teaching him in what light the tyrant should appear to his subjects: far from being a naive expression of a naive belief in virtuous tyrants, it is rather a prudently presented lesson in political prudence.[66] Simonides goes so far as to avoid in this context the very term "tyrant." [67] On the other hand, he now uses the terms "noble" as well as "good" and "useful" much more frequently than ever before, while speaking considerably less of the "pleasant." With a view to the difficulty of appealing directly from the pleasant to the noble, however, he stresses for the time being the "good" (with its "utilitarian" implications) considerably more than the "noble" or "fair." [68] Furthermore, he shows that striving for honor is perfectly compatible with being the subject of a tyrant, thus blotting out completely the odious implications of his previous statement about honor. He shows, too, that honoring subjects by means of prizes is an excellent bargain.[69] And what is most important, he strongly (but by implication) advises against disarming the citizens when he suggests that prizes be offered them for certain achievements of a military nature.[70]

Only after all these steps have been taken does there appear some agreement between Hiero and Simonides on the subject of tyranny. Only now is Hiero prepared, not only to listen to Simonides' advice, but to address to him a question, his only question, concerning the proper conduct of tyrannical government. The formulation of the question shows that he has learned something: he does not speak any longer of "tyrant," but of "ruler." The purport of the question is established by these facts: First, that Simonides had not said anything about the mercenaries whom Hiero had described in his preceding statement as an oppressive burden on the citizens;[71] and second, that Simonides' speech might seem to imply a suggestion that the mercenaries be replaced by citizens. Accordingly, Hiero's question consists of two parts. First, he asks Simonides to advise him how he could avoid incurring hatred on account of his employing mercenaries. Then he asks him whether he means that a ruler who has gained affection is no longer in need of a bodyguard.[72] Simonides answers emphatically that a bodyguard is indispensable:[73] the improvement of tyrannical government should not go to the extreme of undermining the very pillar of tyrannical rule. Thus Simonides' answer to Hiero's only question is tantamount to strong counsel against the abdication which he had tentatively suggested earlier. Besides, Hiero's question as to whether a bodyguard might not be dispensed with might have been prompted by his desire to save the enormous expenses involved. With a view to this possibility, Simonides' statement implies the answer that such expenses are indeed inevitable, but that the proper use of the mercenaries will dispose the subjects to pay the cost of them most cheerfully.[74] Yet, Simonides says, adding a word of advice for which he had not been asked, while the ample use of prizes and the proper use of the mercenaries will help greatly in the solution of the tyrant's financial problems, a tyrant ought not to hesitate to spend his own money for the common good.[75] Nay, a tyrant's interests are better served if he spends money for public affairs rather than for his own affairs. In this context Simonides gives the more specific advice—the giving of which may have been the only purpose of Simonides' starting a conversation with Hiero—that a tyrant should not compete with private men in chariot races and the like, but rather should take care that the greatest number of competitors should come from his city.[76] He should compete with other leaders of cities for victory in the noblest and grandest contest, viz., in making his city as happy as possible. By winning that contest, Simonides promises him, he will gain the love of all his subjects, the regard of many cities, the admiration of all men, and many other good things; by surpassing his friends in acts of kindness he will be possessed of the noblest and most blessed possession among men: he will not be envied while being happy.[77] With this outlook the dialogue ends. Any answer of the tyrant to the poet's almost boundless promise would have been an anticlimax, and, what would have been worse, it would have prevented the reader from reasonably enjoying the polite silence in which a Greek tyrant, old in crime and martial glory, could listen to a siren-song of virtue.[78]

c. The use of characteristic terms

One may say that "the gist of Xenophon's counsel to despots is that a despot should endeavour to rule like a good king."[1] It is therefore all the more striking that he avoids consistently the very term "king." By avoiding the term "king" in a work destined to teach the art of a tyrant, he complies with the rule of tact which requires that one should not embarrass people by mentioning things from the lack of which they can be presumed to suffer: a tyrant must be presumed to suffer from the lack of a valid title to his position. Xenophon's procedure may have been the model for the apparently opposite, but fundamentally identical device of

Machiavelli who in his *Prince* avoids the term "tiranno": individuals who are called "tiranni" in the *Discourses* and elsewhere are called "principi" in the *Prince*.[2] We may also note the absence of the terms *demos* and *politeia* [3] from the *Hiero*.

As for Simonides in particular, he never uses the term "law." He mentions justice only once, making it clear that he is speaking of that justice only which is required of subjects rather than rulers: justice in business dealings.[4] He never speaks of truth or of falsehood or of deceiving. While laughing is never mentioned by Simonides or by Hiero, Simonides speaks once of καταγελᾶν. This is not insignificant because in the only remark of that kind which occurs in the *Hiero*, Xenophon notes that Simonides made a certain statement—it concerns Hiero's love affairs—"laughingly": Hiero is always serious.[5] Simonides, who never mentions courage (ἀνδρεία),[6] once mentions moderation (σωφροσύνη) which is never mentioned by Hiero. On the other hand, Hiero uses the terms μέτριος, κόσμιος, and ἀκρατής which are never used by Simonides.[7]

Some consideration should also be given the distribution of characteristic terms between the two main parts of the dialogue, namely, the indictment of tyranny on the one hand, the suggestions concerning the improvement of tyrannical rule on the other. Terms which are avoided in the second part are: law, free (freedom), nature, courage, misery. On the other hand, moderation is mentioned only in the second part. "Tyrant" (and derivatives) occurs relatively much more frequently in the first part (83 times) than in the second part (7 times); on the other hand, "ruling" (and derivatives) occurs much more frequently in the much shorter second part (12 times) than in the much more extensive first part (4 times): Simonides wants to induce Hiero to think of his position in terms of "ruling" rather than in terms of "tyranny"; for it is not good for any man to think of his activity in odious terms. How well Simonides succeeds is shown by the fact that in his last remark [8] Hiero speaks of "ruler" and no longer of "tyrant." Terms designating pleasure and pain occur relatively much more frequently in the first part (93 times) than in the second part (6 times). On the other hand, "noble" ("fair") and "base" ("ugly") occur relatively much more frequently in the second part (15 times) than in the first part (9 times). The reason is obvious: Simonides wants to educate Hiero to take his bearings by the fair rather than by the pleasant. Χάρις (and derivatives) occurs relatively much more frequently in the second part (9 times) than in the first part (4 times). Ἀνάγκη (and derivatives) occurs relatively more frequently in the second part (9 times) than in the first part (16 times).

IV

THE TEACHING CONCERNING TYRANNY

Since tyranny is essentially a faulty political order, the teaching concerning tyranny necessarily consists of two parts. The first part has to make manifest the specific shortcomings of tyranny ("pathology"), and the second part has to show how these shortcomings can be mitigated ("therapeutics"). The bipartition of the *Hiero* reflects the bipartition of the "tyrannical" teaching itself. Now, Xenophon chose to present that teaching in the form of a dialogue, and he had therefore to choose a particular conversational setting. However sound, and even compelling, his reasons may have been, they certainly lead to the result that he has not given us his "tyrannical" teaching in its pure, scientific form, in the form of a treatise. The reader has to add to, and to subtract from, Hiero's and Simonides' speeches in order to lay hold of Xenophon's teaching. That addition and subtraction is not left to the reader's arbitrary decision. It is guided by the author's indications, some of which have been discussed in the preceding chapters. Nevertheless, a certain ambiguity remains, an ambiguity ultimately due, not to the unsolved riddles implied in many individual passages of the *Hiero*, but to the fact that a perfectly lucid and unambiguous connection between content and form, between a general teaching and a contingent event (e.g., a conversation between two individuals) is impossible.

Considering the primarily practical character of the "tyrannical" teaching as a political teaching, it is necessary that one interlocutor, the pupil, should be a tyrant. It is equally necessary that he should be an actual tyrant, not a potential tyrant. If the pupil were only a potential tyrant, the teacher would have to show him how to become a tyrant, and in so doing he would have to teach him injustice, whereas in the case of an actual tyrant the teacher has the much less odious task of showing him a way toward lesser injustice. Seeing that a tyrant (Periander of Corinth) was said to have instituted most of the common devices for preserving tyranny,[1] one might think that the natural teacher of the tyrannical art would be a great tyrant; but preservation of tyranny and correction of tyranny are two different things. Xenophon evidently felt that only a wise man could teach what he considered the tyrannical art, i.e., the art of ruling well as a tyrant, and that a tyrant would not be wise. This leads to the consequence that the wise man who teaches the tyrannical art cannot have learned that art from a tyrant as Socrates, who teaches the economic art, has learned it from an economist. In other words, the wise teacher of the tyrannical art has to teach it by himself, without any assistance, or he has to discover it by himself.[2] Now, the wise man might transmit to his pupil the whole "tyrannical" teaching, i.e., both the indictment of tyranny and the correction of tyranny; but Xenophon apparently thought that a tyrant's indictment of tyranny would be more impressive for the average reader.[3] Finally, the tyrant might start the conversation by complaining to a wise man about a tyrant's sad lot, in order to elicit his advice. This, however, would presuppose that the tyrant would have a wise friend whom he trusts, and that he would consider himself in need of advice.[4] To sum up, the more one considers alternatives to the conversational setting chosen by Xenophon, the more one becomes convinced that his choice was sound.

Yet this choice, however sound and even necessary, leads to the result that Xenophon's indictment of tyranny is presented by a man who is not wise and who has a selfish interest in disparaging tyranny, whereas his praise of tyranny is presented by a wise man who argues in favor of tyranny without an apparent selfish interest. Besides, since the indictment of tyranny precedes the praise of tyranny, the indictment is presented on the basis of insufficient evidence—for Hiero does not take into account the facts or possibilities set forth by Simonides in the latter part of the *Hiero*— whereas the praise of tyranny seems to be voiced *en pleine connaissance de cause*. That is to say, Xenophon could not help being led to giving a greater weight, at least apparently, to the praise of tyranny than to the indictment of tyranny. The question arises whether this is merely the inevitable result of considerations such as those sketched before, or whether it is directly intended.

One might think for a moment that the ambiguity under consideration was caused merely by Xenophon's decision to treat at all in a dialogue the question of the improvement of tyrannical rule : every ambiguity would have been avoided if he had limited himself to indicting tyranny. A comparison of his conversational treatment of tyranny with Plato's, however, shows that this suggestion does not go to the root of the matter. Plato refrained from teaching the tyrannical art and he entrusted his indictment of tyranny to Socrates. The price which he had to pay for this choice was that he had to entrust his praise of tyranny to men who were not wise (Polos, Callicles, and Thrasymachus) and who therefore were openly praising the very injustice of tyranny. To avoid the latter inconvenience, Xenophon had to pay the price of burdening a wise man with the task of praising tyranny. An effective conversational treatment of tyranny which is free from inconveniences is impossible. For there are only two possibilities apart from those chosen by Xenophon and Plato : the praise of tyranny by the wise might be succeeded by the indictment of tyranny by the unwise, and the indictment of tyranny by the wise might be succeeded by the praise of tyranny by the unwise; these alternatives are ruled out by the consideration that the wise man ought to have the last word.

It is more appropriate to say that the bearing of Xenophon's praise of tyranny is sufficiently limited, not only by the conversational setting, but above all by the fact that his wise man who praises tyranny makes sufficiently clear the essential shortcomings of tyranny. He describes tyranny at its best, but he lets it be understood that tyranny even at its best suffers from serious defects. This implied criticism of tyranny is much more convincing than Hiero's passionate indictment which serves a selfish purpose and which would be literally true only of the very worst kind of tyranny. To see the broad outline of Simonides' criticism of tyranny at its best, one has only to consider the result of his suggested correction of tyranny in the light of Xenophon's, or Socrates', definition of tyranny. Tyranny is defined in contradistinction to kingship : kingship is such rule as is exercised over willing subjects and is in accordance with the laws of the cities; tyranny is such rule as is exercised over unwilling subjects and accords, not with laws, but with the will of the ruler.[5] This definition covers the common form of tyranny, but not tyranny at its best. Tyranny at its best, tyranny as corrected according to Simonides' suggestions, is no longer rule over unwilling subjects. It is most certainly rule over willing subjects.[6] But it remains rule "not according to laws," i.e., it is absolute government. Simonides, who extols tyranny at its best, refrains from using the very term "law."[7] Tyranny is essentially rule without laws, or, more precisely, monarchic rule without laws.

Before considering the shortcomings of tyranny thus understood, we may dwell for a moment on its positive qualities. As regards the tyrant himself, Simonides asserts without hesitation that he may be perfectly happy. Furthermore, he leaves no doubt that the tyrant may be virtuous, and in fact of outstanding virtue. The correction of tyranny consists in nothing else than the transformation of the unjust or vicious tyrant who is more or less unhappy into a virtuous tyrant who is happy.[8] As for the tyrant's subjects, or his city, Simonides makes it clear that it may be very happy. The tyrant and his subjects may be united by the bonds of mutual kindness. The subjects of the virtuous tyrant are treated, not like little children, but like comrades or companions.[9] They are not deprived by him of honors.[10] They are not disarmed; their military spirit is encouraged.[11] Nor are the mercenaries, without whom tyranny is impossible, undesirable from the point of view of the city: they enable the city to wage war vigorously.[12] When Simonides recommends that the tyrant should make a most ample use of prizes and that he should promote agriculture and commerce, if agriculture to a higher degree than commerce, he simply seems to approve of policies which Xenophon considered to befit a well-ordered commonwealth. He thus creates the impression that according to Xenophon tyrannical government can live up to the highest political standards.[13]

Simonides' praise of beneficent tyranny, which at first sight seems to be boundless and rhetorically vague, proves on closer examination to be most carefully worded and to remain within very precise limits. Just as Simonides avoids in it the term "law," he avoids in it the term "freedom." The practical consequence of the absence of laws, he gives us to understand, is the absence of freedom: no laws, no liberty. All specific suggestions made by Simonides flow from this implied axiom, or reveal their political meaning in its light. For instance, when recommending to the tyrant that he consider the citizens as companions or comrades, he does not mean that the tyrant should treat the citizens as his equals, or even as freemen. For slaves may be companions as well as freemen. Furthermore, Simonides advises the tyrant that he consider the citizens as companions, and his friends as his own children: [14] if his very friends are then in every respect his subordinates, the citizens will be his subordinates in a still more far-reaching sense. The advice just referred to shows in addition that Simonides does not go so far in his praise of beneficent tyranny as to call it "paternal" rule.[15] It is true, the subjects of the beneficent tyrant are not disarmed; but in time of peace at least they do not protect themselves against the slaves and evildoers as the citizens of free commonwealths do; they are protected by the tyrant's bodyguard.[16] They are literally at the mercy of the tyrant and his mercenaries, and they can only wish or pray that the tyrant will become, or remain, beneficent. The true character of tyranny even at its best is clearly indicated by Simonides' "Machiavellian" suggestion that the tyrant should do the gratifying things (such as the awarding of prizes) himself, while entrusting to others the punitive actions.[17] It is hardly necessary to say that the tyrant's refraining from openly taking responsibility for punitive action does not bespeak a particular mildness of his rule: Non-tyrannical rulers take that responsibility without any concealment[18] because their authority, deriving from law, is secure. Similarly, the extraordinarily ample use of prizes, especially for the promotion of agriculture, seems to serve the "tyrannical" purpose of keeping the subjects busy with their private concerns rather than with public affairs.[19] At the same time it compensates for the lack of the natural incentives to increase one's wealth, a lack due to the precarious character of property rights under a tyrant. The best tyrant would consider his fatherland his estate. This may be preferable to his impoverishing his fatherland in order to increase his private estate; yet it certainly implies that the best tyrant would consider his fatherland his private property which he would naturally administer according to his own discretion. Thus no subject of a tyrant could have any property rights against the tyrant. The subjects would pay as much as he deems necessary in the form of gifts or voluntary contributions.[20] Nor can the tyrant be said to honor the citizens because he awards prizes or distinctions to some of them; he may be able and willing to enrich his subjects: he cannot accord to them the "equality of honor" which is irreconcilable with tyrannical rule and from the lack of which they may be presumed always to suffer.[21]

These shortcomings of tyranny at its best are not, however, necessarily decisive. How Simonides, and Xenophon, judged of the value of tyranny at its best depends on what they thought of the importance of freedom. As for Simonides, he seems to esteem nothing as highly as honor or praise; and of praise he says that it will be the more pleasant the freer are those who bestow it.[22] This leads to the consequence that the demands of honor or praise cannot be satisfied by tyranny however perfect. The tyrant will not enjoy honor of the highest kind because his subjects lack freedom, and on the other hand the tyrant's subjects will not enjoy full honor for the reason mentioned before. As for Xenophon himself, we have to start from the facts that freedom was considered the aim of democracy, as particularly distinguished from aristocracy, the aim of which was said to be virtue;[23] and that Xenophon was not a democrat. Xenophon's view is reflected in Hiero's implicit assertion that the wise are not concerned with freedom.[24] To establish Xenophon's attitude towards tyranny at its best as characterized by Simonides, we have to consider the relation of tyranny at its best, not to freedom, but to virtue. Only if virtue were impossible without freedom, would the demand for freedom be absolutely justified from Xenophon's point of view.

The term "virtue" occurs five times in the *Hiero*. In only two out of the five cases is it applied to human beings.[25] Only once is it applied to the tyrant. Never is it applied to the tyrant's subjects. Simonides advises the tyrant to be proud of "the happiness of his city" rather than of "the virtue of his chariot horses": he does not mention the virtue of the city as a possible goal of tyrannical rule. It is safe to say that a city ruled by a tyrant is not supposed by him to "practice gentlemanliness as a matter of public concern." [26] But, as has been proved by Socrates' life, there are virtuous men in cities which do not "practise gentlemanliness as a matter of public concern." It is therefore an open question whether and how far virtue is possible under a tyrant. The beneficent tyrant would award prizes for "prowess in war" and for "justice in contractual relations":[27] he would not be concerned with fostering prowess simply and justice simply. This confirms Hiero's assertion that the brave and the just are not desirable as subjects of a tyrant.[28] Only a qualified, or reduced, form of courage and justice befits the subjects of a tyrant. For prowess simply is closely akin to freedom, or love of freedom,[29] and justice simply is obedience to laws. The justice befitting the subjects of a tyrant is the least political form of justice, or that form of justice which is most remote from public-spiritedness: the justice to be observed in contractual, private relations.[30]

But how can a virtuous man—and Simonides' beneficent tyrant would seem to be a virtuous man—rest satisfied with the necessity of preventing his subjects from reaching the summit of virtue? Let us then reconsider the facts mentioned in the preceding paragraph. As regards the fact that Simonides ascribes to the tyrant's subjects a qualified form of prowess only, and fails to ascribe courage to them, we have to remember that in Xenophon's two lists of the virtues of Socrates, courage does not occur.[31] As regards Simonides' failure to ascribe to the tyrant's subjects justice simply, we have to remember that justice can be understood as a part of moderation and that, according to an explicit statement of Simonides, the tyrant's subjects may very well possess moderation.[32] As regards Simonides' failure to ascribe to the tyrant's subjects virtue as such, we have to remember that virtue is not necessarily a generic term, but may indicate a specific virtue distinguished from justice in particular.[33] However this may be, the question of what Simonides thought about the possibility of virtue under tyrannical rule seems to be definitely settled by an explicit statement of his according to which "gentlemen" may live, and live happily, under a beneficent tyrant.[34] In order not to misinterpret Simonides' ascribing to the tyrant's subjects only qualified forms of courage and justice, we have to compare it with Xenophon's failure, in his *Lacedaemoniorum respublica,* to ascribe justice in any sense to the Spartans themselves. The utmost one is entitled to say is that the virtue possible under a tyrant will have a specific color, a color different from that of republican virtue. It may tentatively be suggested that the place occupied within republican virtue by courage is occupied within the virtue befitting the subjects of the excellent tyrant by moderation which is produced by fear.[35] But one has no right to assume that the virtue befitting the subjects of a good tyrant is meant to be inferior in dignity to republican virtue. How little Xenophon believed that virtue is impossible without freedom is shown most strikingly by his admiration for the younger Cyrus whom he does not hesitate to describe as a "slave." [36]

If gentlemen can live happily under a beneficent tyrant, tyranny as corrected according to Simonides' suggestions might seem to live up to Xenophon's highest political standard. To see at once that this is the case, one merely has to measure Simonides' excellent tyrant by the criterion set forth in Xenophon's, or Socrates', definition of the good ruler. The virtue of the good ruler consists in making happy those whom he rules. The aim of the good ruler can be achieved by means of laws—this was done, according to Xenophon, in the most remarkable manner in Lycurgus' city—or by rule without laws, i.e., by tyranny: the beneficent tyrant as described by Simonides makes his city happy.[37] It is certainly most significant that, as regards the happiness achieved by means of laws, Xenophon can adduce an actual example (Sparta), whereas as regards the happiness achieved by tyranny, he offers no other evidence than the promise of a poet. In other words, it is of very great importance that, according to Xenophon, the aim of the good ruler is much more likely to be achieved by means of laws than by means of absolute rule. This does not do away, however, with the admission that, as a matter of principle, rule of laws is not essential for good government.

Xenophon does not make this admission in so many words.

He presents Simonides as describing tyranny at its best and as declaring that the tyrant can make his city happy. Considering the situation in which Simonides expounds his views of tyranny, the objection is justified that what he says serves the purpose of comforting a somewhat disturbed tyrant or at any rate is said *ad hominem* and ought not to be taken as expressing directly Xenophon's own views. We have therefore to consider whether the thesis that tyranny can live up to the highest political standard is defensible on the basis of Xenophon's, or Socrates', political philosophy.

To begin with, it must appear most paradoxical that Xenophon should have had any liking whatsoever for tyranny however good. Tyranny at its best is still rule without laws and, according to Socrates' definition, justice is identical with legality or obedience to laws.[38] Thus tyranny in any form seems to be irreconcilable with the requirement of justice. On the other hand, tyranny would become morally possible if the identification of "just" and "legal" were not absolutely correct, or if "everything according to law were (only) *somehow* (πως) just." [39] The laws which determine what is legal are the rules of conduct upon which the citizens have agreed.[40] "The citizens" may be "the multitude" or "the few"; "the few" may be the rich or the virtuous. That is to say, the laws, and hence what is legal, depend on the political order of the community for which they are given. Should Xenophon or his Socrates have believed that the difference between laws depending on a faulty political order and laws depending on a good political order is wholly irrelevant as far as justice is concerned? Should they have believed that rules prescribed by a monarch, i.e., not by "the citizens," cannot be laws? [41] Besides, is it wholly irrelevant for justice whether what the laws prescribe is reasonable or unreasonable, good or bad? Finally, is it wholly irrelevant for justice whether the laws enacted by the legislator (the many, the few, the monarch) are forcibly imposed on, or voluntarily agreed to by, the other members of the community? Questions such as these are not raised by Xenophon, or his Socrates, but only by Xenophon's young and rash Alcibiades who, however, was a pupil of Socrates at the time when he raised those questions; only Alcibiades, and not Socrates, is presented by Xenophon as raising the Socratic question, "What is law?"[42] Socrates' doubt of the unqualified identification of justice and legality is intimated, however, by the facts that, on the one hand, he considers an enactment of the "legislator" Critias and his fellows a "law" which, he says, he is prepared to obey; and that, on the other hand, he actually disobeys it because it is "against the laws."[43] But apart from the consideration that the identification of "just" and "legal" would make impossible the evidently necessary distinction between just and unjust laws, there are elements of justice which necessarily transcend the dimension of the legal. Ingratitude, e.g., while not being illegal, is unjust.[44] The justice in business dealings—Aristotle's commutative justice proper—which is possible under a tyrant, is for this very reason not essentially dependent on law. Xenophon is thus led to suggest another definition, a more adequate definition, of justice. According to it, the just man is a man who does not hurt anyone, but helps everyone who has dealings with him. To be just, in other words, simply means to be beneficent.[45] If justice is then essentially trans-legal, rule without laws may very well be just: beneficent absolute rule is just. Absolute rule of a man who knows how to rule, who is a born ruler, is actually superior to the rule of laws, in so far as the good ruler is "a seeing law,"[46] and laws do not "see," or legal justice is blind. Whereas a good ruler is necessarily beneficent, laws are not necessarily beneficent. To say nothing of laws which are actually bad and harmful, even good laws suffer from the fact that they cannot "see." Now, tyranny is absolute monarchic rule. Hence the rule of an excellent tyrant is superior to, or more just than, rule of laws. Xenophon's realization of the problem of law, his understanding of the essence of law, his having raised and answered the Socratic question, "What is law?" enables and compels him to grant that tyranny may live up to the highest political standard. His giving, in the *Hiero,* a greater weight to the praise of tyranny than to the indictment of tyranny is then more than an accidental consequence of his decision to present the teaching concerning tyranny in the form of a dialogue.

Yet Simonides goes much beyond praising beneficent tyranny:

he praises in the strongest terms the hoped-for beneficent rule of
a tyrant who previously had committed a considerable number of
crimes. By implication he admits that the praiseworthy character
of tyranny at its best is not impaired by the unjust manner in
which the tyrant originally acquired his power or in which he
ruled prior to his conversion. Xenophon would have been prevented from fully agreeing with his Simonides regarding tyranny
if he had been a legitimist or constitutionalist. Xenophon's
Socrates makes it clear that there is only one sufficient title to
rule: only knowledge, and not force and fraud or election, or,
we may add, inheritance makes a man a king or ruler. If this
is the case, "constitutional" rule, rule derived from elections in
particular, is not essentially more legitimate than tyrannical rule,
rule derived from force or fraud. Tyrannical rule as well as "constitutional" rule will be legitimate to the extent to which the
tyrant or the "constitutional" rulers will listen to the counsels of
him who "speaks well" because he "thinks well." At any rate,
the rule of a tyrant who, after having come to power by means
of force and fraud, or after having committed any number of
crimes, listens to the suggestions of reasonable men, is essentially
more legitimate than the rule of elected magistrates who refuse to
listen to such suggestions, i.e., than the rule of elected magistrates
as such. Xenophon's Socrates is so little committed to the cause
of "constitutionalism" that he can describe the sensible men who
advise the tyrant as the tyrant's "allies." That is to say, he con-
ceives of the relation of the wise to the tyrant in almost exactly
the same way as does Simonides.[47]

While Xenophon seems to have believed that beneficent
tyranny or the rule of a tyrant who listens to the counsels of the
wise is, as a matter of principle, preferable to the rule of laws or
to the rule of elected magistrates as such, he seems to have thought
that tyranny at its best could hardly, if ever, be realized. This is
shown most clearly by the absence of any reference to beneficent
and happy tyrants who actually existed, not only from the *Hiero*,
but from the *Corpus Xenophonteum* as a whole. It is true, in
the *Education of Cyrus* he occasionally refers to a tyrant who was
apparently happy;[48] he does not say, however, that he was benef-

icent or virtuous. Above all, the monarch in question was not a
Greek: the chances of tyranny at its best seem to be particularly
small among Greeks.[49] The reason why Xenophon was so sceptical
regarding the prospects of tyranny at its best is indicated by a
feature common to the two thematic treatments of tyranny at
its best which occur in his works. In the *Hiero* as well as in the
Memorabilia, the tyrant is presented as a ruler who needs guidance by another man in order to become a good ruler: even the
best tyrant is, as such, an imperfect, an inefficient ruler.[50] Being
a tyrant, being called a tyrant and not a king, means having been
unable to transform tyranny into kingship, or to transform a title
which is generally considered defective into a title which is generally
considered valid.[51] The ensuing lack of unquestioned authority
leads to the consequence that tyrannical government is essentially
more oppressive and hence less stable than non-tyrannical government. Thus no tyrant can dispense with a bodyguard which
is more loyal to him than to the city and which enables him to
maintain his power against the wishes of the city.[52] Reasons such
as these explain why Xenophon, or his Socrates, preferred, for all
practical purposes, at least as far as Greeks were concerned, the rule
of laws to tyranny, and why they identified, for all practical purposes, the just with the legal.

The "tyrannical" teaching—the teaching which expounds the
view that a case can be made for beneficent tyranny, and even for
a beneficent tyranny which was originally established by force or
fraud—has then a purely theoretical meaning. It is not more than
a most forceful expression of the problem of law and legitimacy.
When Socrates was charged with teaching his pupils to be "tyrannical," this doubtless was due to the popular misunderstanding of
a theoretical thesis as a practical proposal. Yet the theoretical
thesis by itself necessarily prevented its holders from being un-
qualifiedly loyal to Athenian democracy, e.g., for it prevented
them from believing that democracy is simply the best political
order. It prevented them from being "good citizens" (in the
precise sense of the term)[53] under a democracy. Xenophon does
not even attempt to defend Socrates against the charge that he
led the young to look down with contempt on the political order

established in Athens.[54] It goes without saying that the theoretical thesis in question might have become embarrassing for its holder in any city not ruled by a tyrant, i.e., in almost every city. Socrates' and Xenophon's acceptance of the "tyrannical" teaching would then explain why they became suspect to their fellow-citizens, and, therefore, to a considerable extent, why Socrates was condemned to death and Xenophon was condemned to exile.

It is one thing to accept the theoretical thesis concerning tyranny; it is another thing to expound it publicly. Every written exposition is to a smaller or larger degree a public exposition. The *Hiero* does not expound the "tyrannical" teaching. But it enables, and even compels, its reader to disentangle that teaching from the writings in which Xenophon speaks in his own name or presents the views of Socrates. Only if read in the light of the question posed by the *Hiero* do the relevant passages of Xenophon's other writings reveal their full meaning. The *Hiero* reveals, however, if only indirectly, the conditions under which the "tyrannical" teaching may be expounded. If the city is essentially the community kept together and ruled by law, the "tyrannical" teaching cannot exist for the citizen as citizen. The ultimate reason why the very tyrant Hiero strongly indicts tyranny is precisely that he is at bottom a citizen.[55] Accordingly, Xenophon entrusted the only explicit praise of tyranny which he ever wrote to a "stranger," a man who does not have citizen responsibilities and who, in addition, voices the praise of tyranny not publicly but in a strictly private conversation with a tyrant, and for a purpose which supplies him with an almost perfect excuse. Socrates did not consider it good that the wise man should be simply a stranger;[56] Socrates was a citizen-philosopher. He could not, therefore, with propriety be presented as praising tyranny under any circumstances. There is no fundamental difference in this respect between Xenophon and Plato. Plato entrusted his discussion of the problematic character of the "rule of laws" to a stranger: Plato's Socrates is as silent about this grave, not to say awe-inspiring, subject as is Xenophon's Socrates.[57] Simonides fulfills in the *Corpus Xenophonteum* a function comparable to that fulfilled in the *Corpus Platonicum* by the stranger from Elea.

V

THE TWO WAYS OF LIFE

The primary subject of the conversation described in the *Hiero* is not the improvement of tyrannical government, but the difference between tyrannical and private life with regard to human enjoyments and pains. The question concerning that difference is identical, in the context, with the question as to whether tyrannical life is more choiceworthy than private life or *vice versa*. In so far as "tyrant" is eventually replaced by "ruler," and the life of the ruler is the political life in the strict sense,[1] the question discussed in the *Hiero* concerns the relative desirability of the life of the ruler, or of political life, on the one hand, and of private life on the other. But however the question discussed in the dialogue may be formulated, it is in any case only a special form of the fundamental Socratic question of how man ought to live, or of what way of life is the most choiceworthy.[2]

In the *Hiero,* the difference between the tyrannical and the private life is discussed in a conversation between a tyrant and a private man. This means that the same subject is presented in two different manners. It is presented most obviously by the explicit and thematic statements of the two characters. Yet none of the two characters can be presumed to have stated exactly what Xenophon thought about the subject. In addition, the two characters cannot be presumed to have stated exactly what they themselves thought about it: Hiero is afraid of Simonides, and Simonides is guided by a pedagogic intention. Xenophon presents his view more directly, although less obviously, by the action of the dialogue, by what the characters silently do and unintentionally or occasionally reveal, or by the actual contrast as conceived by him between the tyrant Hiero and the private man Simonides. In so far as Hiero reveals himself as a citizen in the most radical sense and Simonides proves to be a stranger in the most radical

63

sense, the dialogue presents the contrast between the citizen and the stranger. At any rate, Simonides is not a "private man" simply,[3] and he is not an ordinary representative of private life. However silent he may be about his own way of life, he reveals himself by his being or by deed as a wise man. If one considers the conversational setting, the dialogue reveals itself as an attempt to contrast the tyrannical life, or the life of the ruler, not simply with private life, but with the life of the wise man.[4] Or, more specifically, it is an attempt to contrast an educated tyrant, a tyrant who admires, or wishes to admire, the wise, with a wise man who stoops to converse with tyrants.[5] Ultimately, the dialogue serves the purpose of contrasting *the* two ways of life: the political life and the life devoted to wisdom.[6]

One might object that according to Xenophon there is no contrast between the wise man and the ruler: the ruler in the strict sense is he who knows to rule, who possesses the most noble kind of knowledge, who is able to teach what is best; and such knowledge is identical with wisdom.[7] Even if this objection were not exposed to any doubts, there would still remain the difference between the wise man or ruler who wishes to rule or does actually rule, and the wise man or ruler (e.g., Socrates and the poet Simonides) who does not wish to rule and does not engage in politics, but leads a life of privacy and leisure.[8]

The ambiguity that characterizes the *Hiero* is illustrated by nothing more strikingly than by the fact that the primary question discussed in the work does not receive a final and explicit answer. To discover the final answer that is implicitly given, we have to start from the explicit, if provisional, answers. In discussing both the explicit or provisional and the implicit or final answers, we have to distinguish between the answers of the two characters; for we have no right to assume that Hiero and Simonides are in agreement.

Hiero's explicit answer is to the effect that private life is absolutely preferable to tyrannical life.[9] But he cannot deny Simonides' contention that tyrants have greater power than private men to do things by means of which men gain love, and he spontaneously praises being loved more highly than anything else. It is

THE TWO WAYS OF LIFE

true, he retorts that tyrants are also more likely to incur hatred than private men; but Simonides succeeds in silencing this objection by implicitly distinguishing between the good or prudent and the bad or foolish tyrant. In his last utterance, Hiero grants that a ruler or tyrant may gain the affection of his subjects.[10] If one accepts Hiero's premise that love, i.e., being loved, is the most choiceworthy thing, one is led by Simonides' argument to the conclusion that the life of a beneficent tyrant is preferable in the most important respect to private life. As the conclusion follows from Hiero's premise and is eventually not contested by him, we may regard it as his final answer.

Since Hiero is less wise, or competent, than Simonides, his answer is much less important than the poet's. Simonides asserts first that tyrannical life is superior to private life in every respect. He is soon compelled, or able, to admit that tyrannical life is not superior to private life in every respect. But he seems to maintain that tyrannical life is superior to private life in the most important respect: he praises nothing as highly as honor, and he asserts that tyrants are honored above other men.[11] With a view to his subsequent distinction between the good and the bad tyrant, we may state his final thesis as follows: the life of the beneficent tyrant is superior to private life in the most important respect. Simonides and Hiero seem to reach the same conclusion by starting from different premises.

On closer examination, it appears, however, that Simonides' praise of the tyrannical life is ambiguous. In order to lay hold of his view, we have to distinguish in the first place between what he explicitly says and what Hiero believes him to say.[12] Secondly, we have to distinguish between what Simonides says in the first part of the *Hiero* in which he hides his wisdom, and what he says in the second part to which he contributes so much more than to the first part, and in which he speaks no longer as a somewhat diffident pupil but with the confidence of a teacher. We have to attach particular weight to the fact that Simonides' most emphatic statement regarding the superiority of tyrannical life occurs in the first section in which he hides his wisdom to a higher degree than in any subsequent section.[13]

Simonides states to begin with that tyrants experience many more pleasures of all kinds and many fewer pains of all kinds than private men. He grants soon afterwards that in a number of minor respects, if not in all minor respects, private life is preferable to tyrannical life. The question arises whether he thus simply retracts or merely qualifies the general statement made at the beginning: Does he believe that tyrannical life is superior to private life in the most important respect? He never answers this question explicitly. When comparing tyrannical and private life with regard to things more important than bodily pleasures, he uses much more reserved language than he did in his initial and general assertion. In particular, when speaking about honor, he says, after having enumerated the various ways in which people honor tyrants: "for these are of course the kinds of things that subjects do for the tyrants and to *anyone else* whom they happen to honor at the moment." By this he seems to say that the most outstanding honor is not a preserve of tyrants. On the other hand, he says almost immediately thereafter that "you (*sc.* the tyrants) are honored above (all) other men." What he says in the first part of the dialogue might well appear to be ambiguous or inconclusive to the detached reader of the *Hiero* as distinguished from the rather disturbed interlocutor Hiero.[14] In the second part he nowhere explicitly says that tyrannical life is superior to private life in regard to the greatest pleasure. He does assert that the life of tyrants is superior to private life in regard to love. But he never says anywhere in the dialogue that love, or friendship, is the most pleasant thing.[15]

To arrive at a more exact formulation of the difficulty, we start again from the crucial fact that Simonides praises nothing as highly as honor. His contribution to the first part culminates in the assertion that the characteristic difference between the species "real man" (ἀνήρ) and the other kinds of living beings, ordinary human beings of course included, consists in the desire for honor which is characteristic of the former, and in the suggestion that the most outstanding honors are reserved for rulers, if not for tyrants in particular. It is true, he declares in the same context that no human pleasure seems to be superior to the pleasure deriving from honor, and he thus seems to grant that other human pleasures might equal it.[16] On the other hand, he nowhere explicitly excludes the possibility that pleasure is not the sole or ultimate criterion. We have already observed that in the second part of the dialogue the emphasis tacitly shifts from the pleasant to the good and the noble.[17] This change reaches its climax in Simonides' final statement (11.7-15). At its beginning he indicates clearly that the noblest and grandest contest among human beings, and hence the victory in it, is reserved for rulers: victory in that contest consists in rendering very happy the city of which one is the chief. He thus leads one to expect that no human being other than a ruler can reach the summit of happiness: can anything rival victory in the noblest and grandest contest? This question is answered in the concluding sentence, according to which Hiero, by becoming the benefactor of his city, would be possessed of the most noble and the most blessed possession to be met with among human beings: he would be happy without being envied. Simonides does not say that the most noble and most blessed possession accessible to human beings is victory in the most noble and most grand contest among them. He does not even say that one cannot become happy without being envied but by making the city which one rules most happy. In the circumstances he had the strongest reasons for praising the beneficent ruler as emphatically, as explicitly as possible. By refraining from explicitly identifying "making one's city most happy" with "the most noble and most blessed possession," he seems to suggest that there are possibilities of bliss outside of, or beyond, the political life. The very phrasing of the last sentence seems to suggest it. The farmers and artisans who do their work well, are content with their lot and enjoy the simple pleasures of life, are at least as likely to be happy without being envied as rich and powerful rulers however beneficent.[18] What is true of the common people is equally true of other types of men, and in particular of that type which seems to be most important in the conversational situation: those who come to display before the tyrant the wise or beautiful or good things which they possess, who share in the amenities of court life and are rewarded with royal munificence.[19] The highest goal which the greatest ruler could reach only after having made the most extraordinary exertions, seems to be within easy reach of every private man.

This interpretation is open to a very strong objection. We shall not insist on the facts that "being happy" in Simonides' final sentence ("while being happy, you will not be envied") might very well mean "being powerful and wealthy" [20] and that tyrants are superior to private men in regard to power and wealth as not even Hiero can deny. For Simonides might have understood by happiness continuous joy or contentment.[21] Suffice it to say that precisely on account of the essential ambiguity of "being happy" the purport of Simonides' final sentence depends decisively on its second part, viz., the expression "you will not be envied." What this expression means for the decision of the crucial issue becomes clear if we remind ourselves of the following facts: that the purpose of the *Hiero* is to contrast the ruler, not simply with private men in general, but with the wise; that *the* representative of wisdom is Socrates; and that Socrates was exposed, and fell victim, to the envy of his fellow-citizens. If the beneficent ruler can be "happy" without being envied, whereas even Socrates' "happiness" was accompanied by envy,[22] the political life, the life of the ruler or of the tyrant, would seem to be unambiguously superior to the life of the wise man. It would seem then that Simonides' praise of tyranny, in spite of his ironical overstatements and his pedagogic intention, is at bottom serious. True happiness—this seems to be Xenophon's thought—is possible only on the basis of excellence or superiority, and there are ultimately only two kinds of excellence—the excellence of the ruler and that of the wise man. All superior men are exposed to envy on account of their excellence. But the ruler, as distinguished from the wise man, is able to do penance for his superiority by becoming the servant of all his subjects: the hardworking and beneficent ruler, and not the retiring wise man, can put envy at rest.[23]

This must be taken with a grain of salt. It goes without saying that the prospect by means of which Simonides attempts to educate Hiero is incapable of fulfillment. Xenophon knew too well that if there are any forms of superiority which do not expose their possessors to envy, political power, however beneficent, would not be one of them. Or, to put it somewhat differently, if it is true that he who wants to receive kindness must first show kindness, it is not certain that his kindness will not be requited with ingratitude.[24] The thought that a superior man who does not successfully hide his superiority would not be exposed to envy is clearly a delusion. It forms the fitting climax of the illusory image of the tyrant who is happy because he is virtuous. Its aptness consists precisely in this: that it makes intelligible the whole illusory image as the momentary illusion of a wise man, i.e., as something more than a noble lie invented for the benefit of an unwise pupil. Being wise, he is most happy and exposed to envy. His bliss would seem to be complete if he could escape envy. If it were true that only experience could fully reveal the character of tyrannical life—it is this assumption on which the explicit argument of the *Hiero* is largely based—the wise man could not be absolutely certain whether the beneficent tyrant would not be beyond the reach of envy. He could indulge the hope that by becoming a beneficent tyrant, i.e., by actually exercising that tyrannical or royal art which flows from wisdom (if it is not identical with wisdom), he would escape envy while retaining his superiority. Simonides' climactic assertion that by acting on his advice Hiero would become happy without being envied intimates the only reason why a wise man could be imagined for a moment to wish to be a ruler or to envy the man who rules well. It thus reveals the truth underlying Hiero's fear of the wise: that fear proves to be based on a misunderstanding of a momentary velleity of the wise. It reveals at the same time the constant preoccupation of Hiero himself: his misunderstanding is the natural outcome of the fact that he himself is greatly tormented by other people's envy of his happiness. It reveals finally the reason why Simonides could not possibly be envious of Hiero. For the irony of Simonides' last sentence consists, above all, in this: that, if *per impossibile* the perfect ruler would escape from envy, his very escape from envy would expose him to envy; by ceasing to be envied by the multitude, he would begin to be envied by the wise. He would be envied for not being envied. Simonides could become dangerous to Hiero only if Hiero followed his advice. Hiero's final silence is a fitting answer to all the implications of Simonides' final statement.

At any rate, the wise are not envious, and the fact that they are envied does not impair their happiness or bliss.[25] Even if they would grant that the life of the ruler is in a certain respect superior to the life of the wise man, they would wonder whether the price which has to be paid for that superiority is worthwhile. The ruler cannot escape envy but by leading a life of perpetual business, care and trouble.[26] The ruler whose specific function is "doing" or "well-doing" has to serve all his subjects. Socrates, on the other hand, whose specific function is "speaking" or discussing, does not engage in discussion except with those with whom he likes to converse. The wise man alone is free.[27]

To sum up, Simonides' final statement does not imply the view that political life is preferable to private life. This conclusion is confirmed by the carefully chosen expression which he uses for describing the character of happiness unmarred by envy. He calls it "the most noble and most blessed possession to be met with among human beings." He does not call it the greatest good. The most noble and most blessed possession for human beings is choiceworthy, but there are other things which are equally or more choiceworthy. It may even be doubted whether it is simply the most choiceworthy "possession." Euthydemus, answering a question of Socrates, says that freedom is a most noble and most magnificent possession for real men and for cities. The older Cyrus says in a speech addressed to the Persian nobility that the most noble and most "political" possession consists in deriving the greatest pleasure from praise. Xenophon himself says to Seuthes that for a real man and in particular for a ruler, no possession is more noble or more splendid than virtue and justice and gentility. Antisthenes calls leisure the most delicate or luxurious possession.[28] Socrates, on the other hand, says that a good friend is the best, or the most all-productive, possession and that no possession is more pleasant for a free human being than agriculture.[29] Xenophon's Simonides agrees with Xenophon's Socrates and in fact with Xenophon himself by failing to describe "happiness unmarred by envy" as the most pleasant possession for human beings or as the most noble possession for real men or simply as the best possession.[30] We need not discuss here how Xenophon conceived of the exact relation between "possession" and "good." It is safe to assume that he used "possession" mostly in its less strict sense according to which a possession is a good only conditionally, i.e., only if the possessor knows how to use it or to use it well.[31] If this is the case, even the possession which is simply best would not be identical with the greatest good. While people in general are apt to identify the best possession with the greatest good, Socrates makes a clear distinction between the two things. According to him, the greatest good is wisdom, whereas education is the greatest good for human beings,[32] and the best possession is a good friend. Education cannot be the greatest good simply, because gods do not need education. Education, i.e., the most excellent education, which is education to wisdom, is the greatest good for human beings, i.e., for human beings as such, for men in so far as they do not transcend humanity by approaching divinity: God alone is simply wise.[33] The wise man or the philosopher who partakes of the highest good will be blessed although he does not possess "the most noble and most blessed possession to be met with among human beings."

The *Hiero* is silent about the status of wisdom. Although most explicit about various kinds of pleasure, it is silent about the specific pleasures of the wise, such as, for example, friendly discussion.[34] It is silent about the way of life of the wise. This silence cannot be explained by the fact that the thematic subject of the dialogue is the comparison of the life of the ruler, not with the life of the wise man, but with private life in general. For the thematic subject of the parallel dialogue, the *Oeconomicus,* is the economist, or the management of the household, and yet its central chapter contains a most striking confrontation of the life of the economist (who is a ruler) with the Socratic way of life. The *Hiero* is reserved about the nature of wisdom because the purpose of the dialogue, or of Simonides, requires that "wisdom" be kept in its ordinary ambiguity. If we consider, however, how profoundly Socrates or Xenophon agree with Simonides regarding tyranny, we may be inclined to impute to Xenophon's Simonides the Socratic view that is nowhere contradicted by Xenophon, according to which wisdom is the highest good. Certainly, what Simonides says in his final statement in praise of the life of the ruler accords perfectly with the Socratic view.

In the *Hiero,* Xenophon indicates his view of wisdom by incidental remarks entrusted to Simonides and by the action of the dialogue. Simonides mentions two ways of "taking care" of things which lead to gratification: teaching the things that are best (or teaching what things are best), on the one hand; and praising and honoring him who executes what is best in the finest manner, on the other. When applying this general remark to rulers in particular, he does not mention teaching at all; he silently limits the ruler's way of taking care which leads to gratification, to praising and honoring, or more specifically to the offering and distributing of prizes. The specific function of the ruler appears to be strictly subordinate to that of the wise man. In the best case imaginable, the ruler would be the one who, by means of honoring, to say nothing of punishing, would put into practice the teaching or the prescriptions of the wise man.[35] The wise man is the ruler of rulers. Similarly, the ruler is supposed merely to encourage the discovery of, or the looking out for, "something good"; he is not supposed to engage in these intellectual activities himself.[36] It deserves mention that the passage in which Simonides adumbrates his view of the relation of wisdom and rule is one of the two chapters in which the very term tyrant is avoided: Simonides describes by the remarks in question not merely the tyrant, but the ruler in general.[37]

The superiority of the wise man to the ruler is brought to light by the action of the dialogue. The tyrannical life, or the life of the ruler, is chosen by Hiero not only prior to the conversation, but again within the conversation itself: he rejects Simonides' veiled suggestion to return to private life. And Hiero proves to be less wise than Simonides, who rejects the political life in favor of the wise man's private life.[38] At the beginning of the conversation, Simonides suggests that not he, but Hiero, has a better knowledge of the two ways of life or their difference. This suggestion does not lack a certain plausibility as long as one understands by the two ways of life the tyrannical life and private life in general; it proves to be simply ironical if it is considered in the light of the setting, i.e., if it is applied to the difference between the life of the ruler and the life of the wise man. For Hiero proves to be ignorant of the life of the wise man and its goal, whereas Simonides knows, not only his own way of life, but the political life as well, as is shown by his ability to teach the art of ruling well. Only Simonides, and not Hiero, is competent to make a choice between the two ways of life.[39] At the beginning, Simonides bows to Hiero's leadership; he even permits Hiero to defeat him. But in the moment of his victory Hiero becomes aware of the fact that far from really defeating Simonides, he has merely prepared his own downfall. The wise man sits leisurely upon the very goal towards which the ruler is blindly and furiously working his way and which he will never reach. At the end, Simonides' leadership is firmly established: the wise man defeats the ruler. This most obvious aspect of the action is a peculiarity of the *Hiero*. In most of Xenophon's dialogues, no change of leadership takes place: Socrates is the leader from the beginning to the end. In Xenophon's Socratic dialogue *par excellence,* the *Oeconomicus,* a change of leadership does occur; but it is a change from the leadership of the wise man (Socrates) to the leadership of the ruler (the economist Ischomachus). Whereas in the *Oeconomicus* the wise man surrenders to the ruler, in the *Hiero* the ruler surrenders to the wise man. The *Hiero,* and not the *Oeconomicus,* reveals by its action the true relation of rule and wisdom. In addition, the *Hiero* is that work of Xenophon which draws our attention most forcefully to the problem of that relation. It can be said to do this for several reasons. In the first place, because its primary subject is the difference between private life and the life of a certain type of ruler. In the second place, because it does contrast a wise man and a ruler more explicitly than any other Xenophontic writing. And finally, the *Hiero's* most obvious practical aim (the improvement of tyranny) is hardly capable of fulfillment, which precludes the possibility that the obvious practical aim of the work coincides with its final

purpose. Here again we may note a profound agreement between Xenophon and Plato. The precise relation between the
philosopher and the political man (i.e., their fundamental difference) is the thematic premise, not of the *Republic* and the
Gorgias in which Socrates as citizen-philosopher is the leading
character, but of the *Politicus* in which a stranger occupies the
central position.

From what has been said it may be inferred that Simonides'
emphatic praise of honor cannot possibly mean that he preferred
honor as such to all other things. After all, his statement on honor
belongs to that part of the dialogue in which he hides his wisdom
almost completely. Besides, its bearing is sufficiently qualified by
the sentences with which it opens and ends.[40] One might even
think to begin with that his praise of honor can be explained
completely by his pedagogic intention. His intention is to show
Hiero, who reveals a remarkable indifference to virtue, a way to
virtuous rule by appealing, not to virtue or the noble, but to the
pleasant; and the pleasure deriving from honor seems to be the
natural substitute for the pleasure deriving from virtue. Yet
Simonides appeals in his teaching primarily not to Hiero's desire
for honor, but to his desire for love. It could not be otherwise
since Hiero had bestowed spontaneously the highest praise not
on honor, but on love. We may take it then that by extolling
honor Simonides reveals his own preferences rather than those of
his pupil [41]: Simonides, and not Hiero, prefers the pleasure deriving from honor to the other pleasures explicitly mentioned by him.
We may even say that of all desires which are natural, i.e., which
"grow" in human beings independently of any education or teaching,[42] he considered the desire for honor the highest because it is
the foundation of the desire for any excellence, be it the excel-
ence of the ruler or that of the wise man.[43]

Whereas Simonides is concerned with honor, he is not concerned with love. Hiero has to demonstrate to him not only that
as regards love tyrants are worse off than private men, but even
that love is a great good and that private men are particularly
loved by their children, parents, brothers, wives, and companions.
In discussing love, Hiero feels utterly unable to appeal to the

poet's experience or previous knowledge as he did when discussing the pleasures of the table and even of sex. He urges him to acquire the rudiments of knowledge regarding love immediately or in the future without being in any way certain that Simonides would wish to acquire them.[44]

Just as desire for honor is characteristic of Simonides, desire for love is characteristic of Hiero.[45] In so far as Hiero represents the ruler and Simonides represents the wise man, the difference between love and honor as interpreted in the *Hiero* will throw some light on Xenophon's view of the difference between the ruler and the wise man. What Xenophon has primarily in mind is not simply the difference between love and honor in general: Hiero desires to be loved by "human beings," i.e., not merely by real men, but by everyone regardless of his qualities, and Simonides is concerned with admiration or praise, not by everybody, but by "those who are free in the highest degree." [46] The desire which Xenophon or his Simonides ascribes to Hiero, or the ruler, is fundamentally the same as the erotic desire for the common people which Plato's Socrates ascribes to Callicles.[47] Only because the ruler has the desire to be loved by "human beings" as such is he able to become the willing servant and benefactor of all his subjects and hence to become a good ruler. The wise man, on the other hand, has no such desire; he is satisfied with the admiration, the praise, the approval of a small minority.[48] It would seem, then, that the characteristic difference between the ruler and the wise man manifests itself in the objects of their passionate interest and not in the character of their passion itself.[49] Yet it is no accident that Simonides is primarily concerned with being praised by the competent minority, and not with being loved by them, whereas Hiero is primarily concerned with being loved by human beings in the mass, and not with being admired by them. The characteristic difference between the ruler and the wise man may therefore be presumed to manifest itself somehow in the difference between love and admiration.

The meaning of this difference is indicated by Simonides in his praise of the beneficent ruler. The beneficent ruler will be loved by his subjects, he will be passionately desired by human beings, he will have earned the affectionate regard of many cities, whereas he will be praised by all human beings and will be admirable in the eyes of all. Everyone present, but not everyone absent, will be his ally, just as not everyone will be afraid that something might happen to him and not everyone will desire to serve him. Precisely by making his city happy, he will antagonize and hurt her enemies who cannot be expected to love him and to extol his victory. But even the enemies will have to admit that he is a great man: they will admire him and praise his virtue.[50] The beneficent ruler will be praised and admired by all men, whereas he will not be loved by all men: the range of love is more limited than that of admiration or praise. Each man loves what is somehow his own, his private possession; admiration or praise is concerned with the excellent regardless of whether it is one's own or not. Love as distinguished from admiration requires proximity. The range of love is limited not only in regard to space, but likewise—although Xenophon's Simonides in his delicacy refrains from even alluding to it—in regard to time. A man may be admired many generations after his death whereas he will cease to be loved once those who knew him well are dead.[51] Desire for "inextinguishable fame," [52] as distinguished from desire for love, enables a man to liberate himself from the shackles of the Here and Now. The beneficent ruler is praised and admired by all men, whereas he is loved mainly by his subjects: the limits of love coincide normally with the borders of the political community, whereas admiration of human excellence knows no boundaries.[53] The beneficent ruler is loved by those whom he benefits or serves on account of his benefits or services,[54] whereas he is admired even by those to whom he has done the greatest harm and certainly by many whom he did not serve or benefit at all: admiration seems to be less mercenary than love. Those who admire the beneficent ruler while loving him do not necessarily make a distinction between their benefactor and the man of excellence; but those who admire him without loving him—e.g., the enemy cities—rise above the vulgar error of mistaking one's benefactor for the man of excellence.[55] Admiration is as much superior to love as the man of excellence is to one's benefactor as such. To express this somewhat differently, love has no criterion of its relevance outside of itself, but admiration has. If admiration does not presuppose services rendered by the admired to the admirer, one is led to wonder whether it presupposes any services, or any prospect of services, by the admired at all. This question is answered explicitly in the affirmative by Hiero, and tacitly in the negative by Simonides.[56] Hiero is right as regards the ruler: the ruler does not gain the admiration of all men but by rendering services to his subjects. Simonides is right as regards the wise man: the wise man is admired, not on account of any services which he renders to others, but simply because he is what he is. The wise man need not be a benefactor at all in order to be admired as a man of excellence.[57] More precisely: the specific function of the ruler is to be beneficent; he is essentially a benefactor; the specific function of the wise man is to understand; he is a benefactor only accidentally. The wise man is as self-sufficient as is humanly possible; the admiration which he gains is essentially a tribute to his perfection, and not a reward for any services.[58] The desire for praise and admiration as distinguished and divorced from the desire for love is the natural foundation for the predominance of the desire for one's own perfection.[59] This is what Xenophon subtly indicates by presenting Simonides as chiefly interested in the pleasures of eating, whereas Hiero appears to be chiefly interested in the pleasures of sex: for the enjoyment of food, as distinguished from sexual enjoyments, one does not need other human beings.[60]

The specific function of the wise man is not bound up with an individual political community: the wise man may live as a stranger. The specific function of the ruler on the other hand consists in rendering happy the individual political community of which he is the chief. The city is essentially the potential enemy of other cities. Hence one cannot define the function of the ruler without thinking of war, enemies, and allies: the city and her ruler need allies, whereas the wise man does not.[61] To the specific functions correspond specific natural inclinations. The born ruler, as distinguished from him who is born to become wise, must have strong warlike inclinations. Hiero mentions the opinion according to which peace is a great good and war a great evil. He does not simply adopt it, however, for he feels too keenly that war affords great pleasures. When enumerating the very great pleasures which private citizens enjoy in war, he assigns the central place to the pleasure which they derive from killing their enemies. He notes with regret that the tyrant cannot have this great pleasure or at least cannot openly show it and boast of the deed. Simonides does not reveal any delight in war or killing. The most he says in favor of war is that Hiero had greatly exaggerated the detrimental effect on appetite and sleep of that fear which fills men's minds before a battle.[62] Not victory in war as such, but the happiness of one's city, is described by him as the goal of the noblest and grandest contest.[63] Hiero's statement about peace and war [64] doubtless serves the purpose of drawing our attention to the particularly close connection between tyranny and war.[65] But a comparison of this passage with what Xenophon tells us about the inclinations of the king Cyrus makes it clear that he considered a streak of cruelty an essential element of the great ruler in general.[66] The difference between the tyrant and the non-tyrannical ruler is ultimately not a simple opposition, but rather that in the case of the tyrant certain elements of the character of the ruler are more strongly developed or less easily hidden than in the case of the non-tyrannical ruler. Nor is it necessarily true that the pleasure which the ruler takes in hurting enemies is surpassed by his desire to be loved by friends. To say nothing of the fact that what Hiero enjoys most in his sexual relations are the quarrels with the beloved one, he apparently prefers "taking from enemies against their will" to all other pleasures.[67] According to him, the tyrant is compelled to free the slaves, but desirous to enslave the free:[68] if he could afford to indulge his desires, everyone would be his slave. Simonides had limited himself to stating that tyrants are most capable of hurting their enemies and helping their friends. When reproducing this statement, Hiero puts a considerably greater weight on "hurting the enemies" than on "helping the friends"; and when discussing it, he implies that Simonides has an interest of his own in helping his friends but none in hurting his enemies: he can easily see Simonides helping his friends; he cannot see him as well hurting his enemies.[69] Since the wise man does not need human beings in the way in which, and to the extent to which, the ruler does, his attitude toward them is free, not passionate, and hence not susceptible of turning into malevolence or hatred. In other words, the wise man alone is capable of justice in the highest sense. When Hiero distinguishes between the wise and the just man, he implies that the just man is the good ruler. Accordingly, he must be presumed to understand by justice political justice, the justice which manifests itself in helping friends and hurting enemies. When Socrates assumes that the wise man is just, he understands by justice trans-political justice, the justice which is irreconcilable with hurting anyone. The highest form of justice is the preserve of those who have the greatest self-sufficiency which is humanly possible.[70]

VI

PLEASURE AND VIRTUE

The *Hiero* almost leads up to the suggestion that tyranny may be perfectly just. It starts from the opinion that tyranny is radically unjust. The tyrant is supposed to reject the just and noble, or virtue, in favor of the pleasant; or, since virtue is human goodness, he is supposed to reject the good in favor of the pleasant. This opinion is based on the general premise that the good and the pleasant are fundamentally different from each other in such a way that the right choice has to be guided by considerations of the good, and not by considerations of the pleasant.[1]

The thesis that tyranny is radically unjust forms the climax of Hiero's indictment of tyranny. That indictment is exaggerated; Hiero simply reproduces without full conviction the gentleman's image of the tyrant.[2] But the very fact that he is capable of using that image for a selfish purpose proves that his thesis is not altogether wrong. Xenophon has taken some pains to make it clear that while Hiero is not as unjust as he declares the tyrant to be, he is remarkably indifferent to virtue. He does not think of mentioning virtue among the greatest goods or the most choice-worthy possessions. At best, he considers virtuous men, i.e., the virtue of others, to be useful. But even the virtue of others is not regarded by him as an object of delight: he does not seek, and never sought, his companions among the virtuous men. Not he, but Simonides, points out the insignificance of bodily pleasures.[3] Only after having been driven into a corner by Simonides does he praise the virtue of the benefactor of human beings with a view to the fact that such virtue is productive of the highest honor and of unimpaired happiness.[4]

In attempting to educate a man of this kind, Simonides has no choice but to appeal to his desire for pleasure. In order to advise Hiero to rule as a virtuous tyrant, he has to show him that the tyrant cannot obtain pleasure, and in particular that kind of pleasure with which Hiero is chiefly concerned, viz., the pleasure deriving from being loved, but by being as virtuous as possible. What he shows Hiero is a way not so much to virtue as to pleasure. Strictly speaking, he does not advise him to become virtuous. He advises him to do the gratifying things himself while entrusting to others the things for which men incur hatred; to encourage certain virtues and pursuits among his subjects by offering prizes; to keep his bodyguard, yet to use it for the benefit of his subjects; and, generally speaking, to be as beneficent to his fellow-citizens as possible. Now, the benefactor of his fellow-citizens is not necessarily a man of excellence or a virtuous man. Simonides does not advise Hiero to practise any of the things which distinguish the virtuous man from the mere benefactor.

A comparison of the *Hiero* with Isocrates' work on the tyrannical art (*To Nicocles*) makes perfectly clear how amazingly little of moral admonition proper there is in the *Hiero*. Simonides speaks only once of the virtue of the tyrant, and he never mentions any of the special virtues (moderation, courage, justice, wisdom, and so on) when speaking of the tyrant. Isocrates, on the other hand, does not tire of admonishing Nicocles to cultivate his mind, to practise virtue, wisdom, piety, truthfulness, meekness, self-control, moderation, urbanity, and dignity; he advises him to love peace and to prefer a noble death to a base life, as well as to take care of just legislation and adjudication; he calls a good counsellor the most useful and most "tyrannical" possession.[5]

If Simonides can be said to recommend virtue at all, he recommends it, not as an end, but as a means. He recommends just and noble actions to the tyrant as means to pleasure. In order to do this, Simonides, or Xenophon, had to have at his disposal a hedonistic justification of virtue. Moreover, Simonides prepares his teaching by starting a discussion of whether tyrannical life is superior to private life from the point of view of pleasure. In discussing this subject, Hiero and Simonides are compelled to examine a number of valuable things from the point of view of pleasure. The *Hiero* could only have been written by a man who had at his disposal a comprehensive hedonistic interpretation of human life.

Expression of essential parts of that hedonistic interpretation

has been entrusted to Simonides who in one of his poems had said:
"For what life of mortals, or what tyranny, is desirable without
pleasure. Without her not even the lasting life of gods is to be
envied." [6] It is difficult to say how Simonides conceived of the
relation between pleasure and virtue except that he cannot have
considered desirable a virtuous life which is devoid of pleasure.
From the verses which he addressed to Scopas, it appears that
he considered virtue essentially dependent on a man's fate: no
one is protected against coming into situations in which he is
compelled to do base things.[7] He gave the advice to be playful
throughout, and not to be entirely serious about anything. Play
is pleasant, and virtue, or gentlemanliness, is the serious thing
par excellence.[8] If a sophist is a man who uses his wisdom for the
sake of gain and who employs arts of deception, Simonides was a
sophist.[9] The way in which he is presented in the *Hiero* does
not contradict what we are told about the historical Simonides.
Xenophon's Simonides is an "economist"; he rejects the gentleman's view of what is most desirable in favor of the view of the
"real man"; he would be capable of going to any length in "contriving something"; and he is free from the responsibility of the
citizen.[10] While he speaks of the noblest and grandest contest and
of the noblest and most blessed possession, he does not speak of
the noblest and grandest, or most splendid possession ("virtue and
justice and gentility"): he reserves his highest praise, not for
virtue, but for happiness unmarred by envy, and, above all, for
honor.[11] The amazingly amoral nature of the tyrannical teaching
embodied in the second part of the *Hiero* as well as the hedonistic
consideration of human things that is given in the first part accord
perfectly with Simonides' character.

Xenophon's Simonides not only has a definite leaning towards
hedonism; he even has at his disposal a philosophic justification for
his views about the importance of pleasure. What he says in his
initial statement about the various kinds of pleasure and pain
reveals a definite theoretical interest in the subject. He divides
all pleasures into three classes: pleasures of the body, pleasures
of the soul, and pleasures common to body and soul. He subdi-
vides the pleasures of the body into those related to a special organ

(eyes, ears, nose, sexual organs) and those related to the whole body. His failure to subdivide the pleasures of the soul may not be due merely to his wish to stress the pleasures of the body in order to present himself as a lover of those pleasures; it may have to be traced also to the theoretical reasons that there are no parts of the soul in the sense in which there are parts of the body and that the pleasures common to men and brutes are more funda-mental and therefore, from a certain theoretical point of view, more important than those characteristic of human beings.[12] He makes it clear that all pleasures and pains presuppose some kind of knowledge, an act of distinction or judgment, a perception of the senses or of thought.[13] He distinguishes the knowledge pre-supposed by every pleasure and pain from the knowledge or per-ception of our pleasure or pain. He does not consider it unim-portant to indicate that whereas we feel our own pleasures and pains, we merely observe those of others. He possibly alludes to a distinction between the δι' οὗ and the ᾧ with regard to pleas-ures and perceptions.[14] When mentioning the pleasure deriving from sleep, he does not limit himself to pointing out that sleep is unambiguously pleasant; he raises in addition the theoretical question of how and by what and when we enjoy sleep; since he feels that he cannot answer this question, he explains why it is so particularly difficult to answer it.

If we understand by hedonism the thesis that the pleasant is identical with the good, Xenophon's Simonides is not a hedonist. Before he ever mentions the pleasant, he mentions the good: he mentions at the very outset "better" knowledge, by which, of course, he does not mean "more pleasant" knowledge.[15] In his enumer-ation of the various kinds of pleasure he makes it clear that he considers the pleasant and the good fundamentally different from each other: the good and the bad things are sometimes pleasant and sometimes painful. He does not explicitly say how he con-ceives of the precise relation between the pleasant and the good.[16] To establish his view on the subject, we have to pay proper atten-tion to the non-hedonistic principle of preference which he recog-nizes when he speaks with emphasis of "(ordinary) human beings" and of "(real) men." First, regarding "human beings," he seems

to make a distinction between such pleasures as are in accordance
with human nature and such pleasures as are against human
nature:[17] the preferable or good pleasures are those which agree
with human nature. Simonides' non-hedonistic principle of preference would then be "what agrees with human nature." Now,
ordinary human beings may enjoy as much pleasure as real men;
yet real men are to be esteemed more highly than ordinary human
beings.[18] Hence, we may define Simonides' non-hedonistic principle of preference more precisely by identifying it with "what
agrees with the nature of real men." Seeing that he praises nothing as highly as honor, and honor is most pleasant to real men
as distinguished from ordinary human beings, we may say that
the ultimate and complete principle of preference to which Simonides refers in the *Hiero* is the pleasure which agrees with the nature
of real men. What he praises most highly is pleasant indeed, but
pleasure alone does not define it sufficiently; it is pleasant on a
certain level, and that level is determined, not by pleasure, but by
the hierarchy of beings.[19] He is then a hedonist only in so far as he
rejects the view that considerations of pleasure are irrelevant for
right choice: the right goal towards which one has to aim, or with
reference to which one has to judge, must be something which is
intrinsically pleasant. This view seems to have been held by the
historical Simonides as is shown by his verses on pleasure quoted
above. We may ascribe the same view to Xenophon's Hiero, who
admits the distinction between the good and the pleasant and who
characterizes friendship, than which he praises nothing more
highly, as both very good and very pleasant.[20]

This qualified hedonism guides Simonides and Hiero in their
examination of a number of valuable things. That examination
leads to the conclusion suggested by Hiero that friendship has a
higher value than city or fatherland or patriotism.[21] Friendship,
i.e., being loved and cared for by the small number of human
beings whom one knows intimately (one's nearest relatives and
companions) is not only "a very great good"; it is also "very
pleasant." It is a very great good because it is intrinsically pleasant. Trust, i.e., one's trusting others, is "a great good." It is not a
very great good, because it is not so much intrinsically pleasant as

the *conditio sine qua non* of intrinsically pleasant relations. A man whom one trusts is not yet a friend: a servant or a bodyguard must be trustworthy, but there is no reason why they ought to be one's friends. While trust is not intrinsically pleasant, it stands in a fairly close relation to pleasure: when discussing trust, Hiero mentions pleasure three times. On the other hand, in the passage immediately following in which he discusses "fatherlands," he does not mention pleasure at all.[22] Not only are "fatherlands" not intrinsically pleasant; they do not even stand in a close relation to pleasure. "Fatherlands are worth very much" because the citizens afford each other protection without pay against violent death and thus enable each citizen to live in safety. That for which the fatherland is "worth very much" is life in safety; safety, or freedom from fear, the spoiler of all pleasures, is the *conditio sine qua non* of every pleasure however insignificant; but to live in safety and to live pleasantly are clearly two different things. More precisely, the fatherland is not, as is trust, the specific condition of the great pleasures deriving from friendship: "strangers," men like Simonides, may enjoy friendship.[23] Friendship and trust are good for human beings as such, but the cities are good primarily, not to say exclusively, for the citizens and the rulers; they are certainly less good for strangers, and still less for slaves.[24] The fatherland, or the city, is good for the citizens because it liberates them from fear. This does not mean that it abolishes fear; it rather replaces one kind of fear (the fear of enemies, evil-doers, and slaves) by another (the fear of the laws or of the law-enforcing authorities).[25] The city, as distinguished from friendship and trust, is not possible without compulsion; and compulsion, constraint, or necessity (ἀνάγκη) is essentially unpleasant.[26] Friendship, i.e., being loved, is pleasant, while being patriotic is necessary.[27] While friendship, as praised by Hiero, is not only pleasant but also good, its goodness is not moral goodness or nobility: Hiero praises him who has friends regardless of whether the friends are morally good or not.[28] In so far as friendship is being loved, preferring friendship to fatherland is tantamount to preferring oneself to others: when speaking about friendship, Hiero is silent about the mutuality to which he explicitly refers

when discussing trust and fatherland. It is tantamount to prefer-
ing one's pleasure to one's duties to others.

The thesis that friendship is a greater good than the fatherland is suggested by Hiero who has a strong motive for asserting
that private life is superior to the life of the ruler which is the
political life *par excellence*. But that thesis is more than a weapon
convenient for Hiero's purpose. Simonides, who could have been
induced by his pedagogic intention rather to prefer fatherland to
friendship, tacitly adopts Hiero's thesis by advising the tyrant to
consider his fatherland as his estate, his fellow-citizens as his comrades, his friends as his children, and his sons as the same thing as
his life or soul.[29] He is even less capable than Hiero of assigning
to the fatherland the most exalted place among the objects of
human attachment. He adopts Hiero's thesis not only "by speech,"
but "by deed" as well: he lives as a stranger; he chooses to live
as a stranger. Contrary to Hiero, he never praises the fatherland
or the city. When he urges Hiero to think of the common good,
and of the happiness of the city, he emphasizes the fact that this
advice is addressed to a tyrant or ruler. Not Simonides, but Hiero,
is concerned with being loved by "human beings" in the mass
and therefore has to be a lover of the city in order to reach his
goal. Simonides desires nothing as much as praise by the small
number of competent judges: he can be satisfied with a small group
of friends.[30] It is hardly necessary to repeat that his spontaneous
praise of honor is concerned exclusively with the benefit of him
who is honored or praised and is silent about the benefits to be
rendered to others or the duties to others.

The view that a non-political good such as friendship is more
valuable than the city was not the view of the citizen as such.[31]
It remains to be considered whether it was acceptable to citizen-
philosophers. Socrates agrees with Hiero as regards the fact that
"the fatherlands are worth very much" because they afford safety,
or protection against injury, to the citizens.[32] Xenophon seems to
indicate by the plan of the *Memorabilia* that Socrates attached a
greater importance to the self than to the city.[33] This is in accordance with Xenophon's distinction between the man of excellence and the benefactor of his fellow-citizens. Xenophon himself

was induced to accompany Cyrus, an old enemy of Athens, on his
expedition against his brother by the promise of Proxenus, an old
guest-friend of his, that he would make him a friend of Cyrus if
he would come. Proxenus, a pupil of Gorgias, of a man who had
no fixed domicile in any city,[34] explicitly stated that he himself
considered Cyrus worth more to him than his fatherland. Xenophon does not say in so many words that he might conceivably
come to consider Cyrus' friendship preferable to his fatherland;
but he certainly was not shocked by Proxenus' statement and he
certainly acted as if he were capable of sharing Proxenus' sentiment. Socrates had some misgivings regarding Xenophon's becoming a friend of Cyrus and he advised him therefore to consult
Apollo about the journey; but Xenophon was so anxious to join
Cyrus or to leave his fatherland that he decided at once to accept
Proxenus' invitation. Even after everything had gone wrong with
Cyrus' expedition, Xenophon was not anxious to return to his
fatherland, although he was not yet exiled. If his comrades had
not passionately protested, he would have founded a city "in some
barbarian place"; not Xenophon, but his opponents, felt that one
ought not to esteem anything more highly than Greece.[35] Later
on, he did not hesitate to accompany Agesilaus on his campaign
against Athens and her allies which culminated in the battle of
Coronea.[36]

Lest we be carried away by blind indignation,[37] we shall try
to understand what we might call Xenophon's theoretical and
practical depreciation of the fatherland or the city [38] in the light
of his political teaching in general and of the teaching of the *Hiero*
in particular. If wisdom or virtue is the highest good, the fatherland or the city cannot be the highest good. If virtue is the
highest good, not the fatherland as such, but only the virtuous
community or the best political order can command a good man's
undivided loyalty. If he has to choose between a fatherland which
is corrupt and a foreign city which is well-ordered, he may be
justified in preferring that foreign city to his fatherland. Precisely because he is a good man, he will not be a good citizen in a
bad polity.[39] Just as in choosing horses one looks for the best,
and not for those which are born in the country, the wise general

will fill the ranks of his army not merely with his fellow-citizens but with every available man who can be expected to be virtuous.[40] In the spirit of this maxim Xenophon himself devoted his most extensive work to an idealizing description of the achievements of the "barbarian" Cyrus.

The reason why the city as such cannot lay claim to man's ultimate attachment is implied in Xenophon's "tyrannical" teaching. We have stated that according to that teaching beneficent tyranny is theoretically superior and practically inferior to rule of laws and legitimate government. In doing so, we might seem to have imputed to Xenophon the misologist view that a political teaching may be "morally and politically false . . . in proportion as (it is) metaphysically true." But a pupil of Socrates must be presumed to have believed rather that nothing which is practically false can be theoretically true.[41] If Xenophon did then not seriously hold the view that beneficent tyranny is superior to rule of laws and legitimate government, why did he suggest it at all? The "tyrannical" teaching, we shall answer, serves the purpose, not of solving the problem of the best political order, but of bringing to light the nature of political things. The "theoretical" thesis which favors beneficent tyranny is indispensable in order to make clear a crucial implication of the practically and hence theoretically true thesis which favors rule of law and legitimate government. The "theoretical" thesis is a most striking expression of the problem, or of the problematic character, of law and legitimacy: legal justice is a justice which is imperfect and more or less blind, and legitimate government is not necessarily "good government" and almost certainly will not be government by the wise. Law and legitimacy are problematic from the highest point of view, namely, from that of wisdom. In so far as the city is the community kept together, nay, constituted, by law, the city cannot so much as aspire to that highest moral and intellectual level attainable by certain individuals. Hence the best city is morally and intellectually on a lower plane than the best individual.[42] The city as such exists on a lower plane than the individual as such. "Individualism" thus understood is at the bottom of Xenophon's "cosmopolitanism."

The emphasis on pleasure which characterizes the argument of the *Hiero* leads to a certain depreciation of virtue. For there is nothing in the dialogue to suggest that Simonides considered virtue intrinsically pleasant. The beneficence or virtue of the good tyrant procures for him the most noble and most blessed possession: it is not itself that possession. Simonides replaces the praise of virtue by a praise of honor. As appears from the context, this does not mean that only virtue can lead to honor. But even if it meant this much, his praise of honor would imply that not virtue, but the reward or result of virtue, is intrinsically pleasant.[43]

Xenophon might seem to have revealed his, or his Socrates', attitude towards hedonism, however understood, in a conversation between Socrates and Aristippus which he has recorded or invented. That conversation is chiefly concerned with the unequivocal connection between love of pleasure and the rejection of the life of a ruler: the pleasure-loving Aristippus goes so far as to prefer explicitly the life of a stranger to political life in any sense. Socrates concludes the conversation by reciting a summary of Prodicus' writing on Hercules in which the pursuit of pleasure is almost identified with vice.[44] This is appropriate only if Aristippus' view is taken to imply a remarkable depreciation of virtue. It is not impossible that the historical Aristippus has served to some extent as a model for Xenophon's Simonides. To say nothing of his hedonistic teaching, he was the first of the Socratics to take pay for his teaching and he could adjust himself to places, times, and men so well that he was particularly popular with the Syracusan tyrant Dionysius.[45]

Be this as it may, the conversation referred to between Socrates and Aristippus tells us very little about Xenophon's attitude towards hedonism. After all, Socrates and Aristippus discuss almost exclusively the pleasures of the body; they barely mention the pleasures deriving from honor or praise. Besides, it would be rash to exclude the possibility that Xenophon's account of that conversation is to a certain extent ironical. That possibility is suggested by the disproportionately ample use which Socrates explicitly makes of an epideictic writing of the sophist Prodicus as an instrument of moral education.[46] Let us not forget the fact that in the only conversation between Socrates and Xenophon which is recorded in the latter's Socratic writings, Xenophon presents himself as a lover of certain sensual pleasures and as being rebuked by Socrates in much more severe terms than Aristippus ever was. This is not surprising, of course, since Xenophon is more explicit than Aristippus in praising the pursuit of sensual pleasure.[47] To point, therefore, to facts which are perhaps less ambiguous, Xenophon no more than his Simonides contends that virtue is the most blessed possession; he indicates that virtue is dependent on external goods and, far from being an end in itself, ought to be in the service of the acquisition of pleasure, wealth, and honors.[48]

At first glance, it is not altogether wrong to ascribe the same view even to Socrates. A distinguished historian did ascribe it, not only to Xenophon's Socrates, but to Plato's as well. "D'une part, son bon sens et sa grande sagesse pratique lui font sentir qu'il doit y avoir un principe d'action supérieur à l'agréable ou au plaisir immédiat; d'autre part, quand il s'efforce de déterminer ce principe lui-même, il ne parvient pas à le distinguer de l'utile, et l'utile lui-même ne diffère pas essentiellement de l'agréable." Yet one cannot leave it at that; one has to acknowledge that Socrates' teaching is characterized by a fundamental contradiction: "Socrate recommande de pratiquer les diverses vertus à cause des avantages matériels qu'elles sont susceptibles de nous procurer; mais ces avantages il n'en jouit jamais."[49] Should Socrates, who insisted so strongly on the indispensable harmony between deed and speech completely have failed to account "by speech" for what he was revealing "by deed"? To solve the contradiction in question, one merely has to remind oneself of the distinction which Xenophon's Socrates makes silently and Plato's Socrates makes explicitly between two kinds of virtue or gentlemanliness: between common or political virtue, whose ends are wealth and honor, and true virtue which is identical with self-sufficient wisdom.[50] The fact that Socrates sometimes creates the impression that he was oblivious of true virtue, or that he mistook common virtue for true virtue, is explained by his habit of leading his discussions, as far as possible, "through the opinions

accepted by human beings." [51] Thus the question of Socrates'
attitude towards hedonism is reduced to the question as to
whether wisdom, the highest good, is intrinsically pleasant. If
we may trust Xenophon, Socrates has disclosed his answer in his
last conversation: not so much wisdom, or true virtue itself,
as one's consciousness of one's progress in wisdom or virtue, affords
the highest pleasure. [52] Thus Socrates ultimately leaves no doubt
as to the fundamental difference between the good and the pleasant. No man can be simply wise; therefore, not wisdom, but
progress towards wisdom is the highest good for man. Wisdom
cannot be separated from self-knowledge; therefore, progress
towards wisdom will be accompanied by awareness of that progress. And that awareness is necessarily pleasant. This whole—
the progress and the awareness of it—is both the best and the
most pleasant thing for man. It is in this sense that the highest
good is intrinsically pleasant. Concerning the thesis that the most
choiceworthy thing must be intrinsically pleasant, there is then
no difference between the historical Simonides, Xenophon's
Simonides, and Xenophon's Socrates, and, indeed, Plato's Socrates.[53] Nor is this all. There is even an important agreement
between Xenophon's Simonides and his Socrates as regards the
object of the highest pleasure. For what else is the pleasant
consciousness of one's progress in wisdom or virtue but one's
reasonable and deserved satisfaction with, and even admiration
of,[54] oneself? The difference between Socrates and Simonides
seems then to be that Socrates is not at all concerned with being
admired or praised by others, whereas Simonides is concerned
exclusively with it. To reduce this difference to its proper pro-
portions, it is well to remember that Simonides' statement on
praise or honor is meant to serve a pedagogical function. The
Hiero does not supply us then with the most adequate formulation of Xenophon's view regarding the relation of pleasure and
virtue. But it is the only writing of Xenophon which has the
merit, and even the function, of posing the problem of that relation in its most radical form: in the form of the question as to
whether the demands of virtue cannot be completely replaced by,
or reduced to, the desire for pleasure, if for the highest pleasure.

VII

PIETY AND LAW

After advising the democratic rulers of Athens how they could overcome the necessity under which they found themselves of acting unjustly, Xenophon reminds them of the limitations of his advice, and, indeed, of all human advice, by giving them the additional advice to inquire of the gods in Dodona and in Delphi whether the reforms suggested by him would be salutary to the city both now and in the future. Yet even divine approval of his suggestions would not suffice. He gives the Athenians the crowning advice, in case the gods should approve of his suggestions, that they further ask the gods to which of the gods they ought to sacrifice in order to be successful. Divine approval and divine assistance seem to be indispensable for salutary political action. These remarks must be of special interest to the interpreter of the *Hiero* on account of the place where they occur in the *Corpus Xenophonteum*, for they occur at the end of the *Ways and Means*.[1] Still, their content cannot be surprising to any reader of our author: pious sentiments are expressed, more or less forcefully, in all those of his writings in which he speaks in his own or in Socrates' name.

One of the most surprising features of the *Hiero*, i.e., of the only work of Xenophon in which he never speaks in the first person, is its complete silence about piety. Simonides never mentions piety. He does not say a word about the advisability of asking any gods whether his suggestions regarding the improvement of tyrannical rule would be salutary. Nor does he remind Hiero of the need of divine assistance. He does not admonish him in any way to worship the gods.[2] Hiero, too, is silent about piety. In particular, when enumerating the various virtues, he was almost compelled to mention piety: he fails to do so.

It might seem that this silence is sufficiently explained by the subject matter of the work. The tyrant, and indeed any absolute ruler, may be said to usurp honors rightfully belonging to the gods alone.[3] Yet the *Hiero* deals, not so much with how tyrants

92

usually live, as with how tyranny can best be preserved or rather improved. If we may believe Aristotle, piety is rather more necessary for preserving and improving tyrannical government than it is for the preservation and improvement of any other political order. We might be inclined to credit Xenophon with the same view, since he indicates that the régime of Cyrus became the more pious in proportion as it became more absolute.[4] But Cyrus is not a tyrant strictly speaking. According to Xenophon, tyranny is in any case rule without laws, and according to his Socrates, piety is knowledge of the laws concerning the gods:[5] where there are no laws, there cannot be piety. However, the identification of piety with knowledge of the laws concerning the gods is not Xenophon's last word on the subject. In his final characterization of Socrates he says that Socrates was so pious that he would do nothing without the consent of the gods. When he describes how Socrates made his companions pious, he shows how he led them to a recognition of divine providence by making them consider the purposeful character of the universe and its parts.[6] It seems, then, that just as he admits a trans-legal justice, although his Socrates identifies justice with legality, so he admits a piety which emerges out of the contemplation of nature and which has no necessary relation to law; a piety, that is, whose possibility is virtually denied by the definition suggested by his Socrates. We shall conclude that the silence of the *Hiero* about piety cannot be fully explained by the subject matter of the work. For a full explanation one would have to consider the conversational situation, the fact that the *Hiero* is a dialogue between an educated tyrant and a wise man who is not a citizen-philosopher.

While the *Hiero* is silent about piety, it is not silent about the gods. But the silence about piety is reflected in what it says, or does not say, about the gods. In the sentence with which he concludes his statement about friendship, Hiero uses an expression which is reminiscent of an expression used in a similar context by Ischomachus in the *Oeconomicus*. Hiero speaks of those who are born by nature, and at the same time compelled by law, to love. Whereas Hiero speaks of a co-operation of nature and law, Ischomachus speaks of a co-operation of the god (or the gods) and law.[7] Hiero replaces "the god" or "the gods" by "nature." Xenophon's Simonides never corrects him. He seems to be the same Simonides who is said repeatedly to have postponed and finally abandoned the attempt to answer the question which Hiero had posed him, What is God?[8] It is true, both Hiero and Simonides mention "the gods," but there is no apparent connection between what they say about "nature" and what they say about "the gods." [9] It is possible that what they mean by "the gods" is chance rather than "nature" or the origin of the natural order.[10]

The practical bearing of the difference between Ischomachus' and Hiero's statements appears from the different ways in which they describe the co-operation of gods or nature and law in the parallel passages cited. Ischomachus says that a certain order which has been established by the gods is at the same time praised by the law. Hiero says that men are prompted by nature to a certain action or feeling, to which they are at the same time compelled by the law. Ischomachus, who traces the natural order to the gods, describes the specific work of the law as praising; Hiero who does not take that step, describes it as compelling. One's manner of understanding and evaluating the man-made law depends then on one's manner of understanding the order which is not man-made and which is only confirmed by the law. If the natural order is traced to the gods, the compulsory character of the law recedes into the background. Conversely, the law as such is less likely to appear as an immediate source of pleasure if one does not go beyond the natural order itself. The law assumes a higher dignity if the universe is of divine origin. The notion linking "praise" and "gods" is gentlemanliness. Praise as distinguished from compulsion suffices for the guidance of gentlemen, and the gods delight at gentlemanliness.[11] As we have seen, Hiero's and Simonides' gentlemanliness is not altogether beyond doubt. Ischomachus, on the other hand, who traces the natural order to the gods and who describes in the cited passage the work of the law as praising, is the gentleman *par excellence*. What the attitude of the citizen-philosopher Socrates was can be ascertained only by a comprehensive and detailed analysis of Xenophon's Socratic writings.

NOTES

INTRODUCTION

1 Compare *Social Research*, v. 13, 1946, pp. 123-124.—Hobbes, *Leviathan*, "A Review and Conclusion" (ed. by A. R. Waller, p. 523): ". . . the name of Tyranny, signifieth nothing more, nor lesse, than the name of Sovereignty, be it in one, or many men, saving that they that use the former word, are understood to be angry with them they call Tyrants. . . ." — Montesquieu, *De l'Esprit des Lois*, XI 9: "L'embarras d'Aristote paraît visiblement quand il traite de la monarchie. Il en établit cinq espèces: il ne les distingue pas par la forme de la constitution, mais par des choses d'accident, comme les vertus ou les vices des princes. . . ."

2 *Principe*, ch. 15, beginning; *Discorsi* I, beginning.

3 The most important reference to the *Cyropaedia* occurs in the *Principe*. It occurs a few lines before the passage in which Machiavelli expresses his intention to break with the whole tradition (ch. 14, towards the end). The *Cyropaedia* is clearly referred to in the *Discorsi* at least four times. If I am not mistaken, Machiavelli mentions Xenophon in the *Principe* and in the *Discorsi* more frequently than he does Plato, Aristotle, and Cicero taken together.

4 *Discorsi* II 2.

5 Classical political science took its bearings by man's perfection or by how men ought to live, and it culminated in the description of the best political order. Such an order was meant to be one whose realisation was possible without a miraculous or non-miraculous change in human nature, but its realisation was not considered probable, because it was thought to depend on chance. Machiavelli attacks this view both by demanding that one should take one's bearings, not by how men ought to live, but by how they actually live, and by suggesting that chance could or should be controlled. It is this attack which laid the foundation for all specifically modern political thought. The concern with a guarantee for the realisation of the "ideal" led to both a lowering of the standards of political life and to the emergence of "philosophy of history": even the modern opponents of Machiavelli could not restore the sober view of the classics regarding the relation of "ideal" and "reality."

I. THE PROBLEM

1 *Hiero* 1.8-10; 2.3-6; 3.3-6; 8.1-7; 11.7-15.

2 *Memorabilia* II 1.21; *Cyropaedia* VIII 2.12.   Compare Aristotle, *Politics* 1325a34 ff. and Euripides, *Phoenissae* 524-5.

3 *Memorabilia* I 2.56.

4 *Hiero* 1.1; 2.5.

5 *Hiero* 8.1. Compare *Memorabilia* IV 2.23-24 with *ib.* 16-17.

6 *Hiero* 1.14-15; 7.2. Compare Plato, *Seventh Letter* 332d6-7 and Isocrates, *To Nicocles* 3-4.

II. THE TITLE AND THE FORM

1 How necessary it is to consider carefully the titles of Xenophon's writings, is shown most clearly by the difficulties which are presented by the titles of the *Anabasis*, of the *Cyropaedia* and, though less obviously, of

the *Memorabilia*. — Regarding the title of the *Hiero*, see also IV note 50 below.

2 There is only one more writing of Xenophon which would seem to serve the purpose of teaching a skill, the π. ἱππικῆς ; we cannot discuss here the question why it is not entitled ʽΙππικός . — The purpose of the *Cyropaedia* is theoretical rather than practical as appears from the first chapter of the work.

3 Compare *Cyropaedia* I 3.18 with Plato, *Theages* 124e11-125e7 and *Amatores* 138b15 ff.

4 *De vectigalibus* 1.1. Compare *Memorabilia* IV 4.11-12 and *Symposium* 4. 1-2.

5 *Hiero* 4.9-11 ; 7.10, 12 ; 8.10 ; 10.8 ; 11.1.

6 *Memorabilia* I 2.9-11 ; III 9.10 ; IV 6.12 (compare IV 4). *Oeconomicus* 21.12. *Resp. Lac.* 10.7 ; 15.7-8. *Agesilaus* 7.2. *Hellenica* VI 4.33-35 ; VII 1.46 (compare V 4.1 ; VII 3.7-8). The opening sentence of the *Cyropaedia* implies that tyranny is the least stable régime. (See Aristotle, *Politics* 1315b10 ff.)

7 *Hiero* 4.5. *Hellenica* V 4.9, 13 ; VI 4.32. Compare *Hiero* 7.10 with *Hellenica* VII 3.7. See also Isocrates, *Nicocles* 24.

8 Plato, *Republic* 393c11.

9 *Memorabilia* III 4.7-12 ; 6.14 ; IV 2.11.

10 *Oeconomicus* 1.23 ; 4.2-19 ; 5.13-16 ; 6.5-10 ; 8.4-8 ; 9.13-15 ; 13.4-5 ; 14.3-10 ; 20. 6-9 ; 21.2-12. The derogatory remark on tyrants at the end of the work is a fitting conclusion for a writing devoted to the royal art as such. Since Plato shares the "Socratic" view according to which the political art is not essentially different from the economic art, one may also say that it can only be due to secondary considerations that his *Politicus* is not entitled *Oeconomicus*.

11 *Memorabilia* IV 6.12.

12 *Apologia Socratis* 34.

13 *Memorabilia* I 2.31 ff. ; III 7.5-6.

14 Plato, *Hipparchus* 228b-c (cf. 229b). Aristotle, *Resp. Athen.* 18.1.

15 Plato, *Second Letter* 310e5 ff.

16 *Memorabilia* I 5.6.

17 Aristophanes, *Pax* 698-9. Aristotle, *Rhetoric* 1391a8-11 ; 1405b24-28. See also Plato, *Hipparchus* 228c. — Lessing called Simonides the Greek Voltaire.

18 *Oeconomicus* 6.4 ; 2.2, 12 ff. Compare *Memorabilia* IV 7.1 with *ib.* III 1.1 ff. Compare *Anabasis* VI 1.23 with *ib.* I 10.12.

19 *Hiero* 9.7-11 ; 11.4, 13-14. Compare *Oeconomicus* 1.15.

20 *Hiero* 1.2, 10 ; 2.6.

21 Note the almost complete absence of proper names from the *Hiero*. The only proper name that occurs in the work (apart, of course, from the names of Hiero, Simonides, Zeus and the Greeks) is that of Daïlochus, Hiero's favorite. — George Grote, *Plato and the other companions of Socrates*, London, 1888, v. I, 222 makes the following just remark : "When we read the recommendations addressed by Simonides, teaching Hiero how he might render himself popular, we perceive at once that they are alike well intentioned and ineffectual. Xenophon could neither find any real Grecian despot corresponding to this portion . . . nor could he invent one with any show of plausibility." Grote continues, however, as follows : "He was forced to resort to other countries and other habits different from those of Greece. To this necessity probably we owe the Cyropaedia." For the moment, it suffices to remark that, according to Xenophon, Cyrus is not a tyrant but a king. Grote's error is due to the identification of "tyrant" with "despot."

[22] Simonides barely alludes to the mortality of Hiero or of tyrants in general (*Hiero* 10.4): Hiero, being a tyrant, must be supposed to live in perpetual fear of assassination. Compare especially *Hiero* 11.7, end, with *Agesilaus* 9.7 end. Compare also *Hiero* 7.2 and 7.7 ff. as well as 8.3 ff. (the ways of honoring people) with *Hellenica* VI 1.6 (honoring by solemnity of burial). Cf. *Hiero* 11.7, 15 with Plato, *Republic* 465d2-e2.

III. THE SETTING

a. The characters and their intentions

[1] *Hiero* 1.12; 2.8. Compare Plato, *Republic* 579b3-c3.

[2] Aristotle, *Rhetoric* 1391a8-11.

[3] *Hiero* 1.13; 6.13; 11.10.

[4] *Memorabilia* I 2.33. *Oeconomicus* 7.2. *Cyropaedia* I 4.13; III 1.14; VIII 4.9.

[5] *Hiero* 1.1-2.

[6] Aristotle, *Politics* 1311a4-5. Compare the thesis of Callicles in Plato's *Gorgias*.

[7] Observe the repeated εἰκός in *Hiero* 1.1-2. The meaning of this indication is revealed by what happens during the conversation. In order to know better than Simonides how the two ways of life differ in regard to pleasures and pains, Hiero would have to possess actual knowledge of both ways of life; i.e., Hiero must not have forgotten the pleasures and pains characteristic of private life; yet Hiero suggests that he does not remember them sufficiently (1.3). Furthermore, knowledge of the difference in question is acquired by means of calculation or reasoning (1.11,3), and the calculation required presupposes knowledge of the different value, or of the different degree of importance, of the various kinds of pleasure and pain; yet Hiero has to learn from Simonides that some kinds of pleasure are of minor importance as compared with others (2.1; 7.3-4). Besides, in order to know better than Simonides the difference in question, Hiero would have to possess at least as great a power of calculating or reasoning as Simonides; yet Simonides shows that Hiero's alleged knowledge of the difference (a knowledge which he had not acquired but with the assistance of Simonides) is based on the fatal disregard of a most relevant factor (8.1-7). The thesis that a man who has experienced both ways of life knows the manner of their difference better than he who has experienced only one of them, is then true only if important qualifications are added; in itself, it is the result of an enthymeme and merely plausible.

[8] *Hiero* 1.8, 14, 16. Simonides says that tyrants are universally admired or envied (1.9), and he implies that the same is of course not true of private men as such. His somewhat more reserved statements in 2.1-2 and 7.1-4 about specific kinds of pleasure must be understood, to begin with, in the light of his general statement about all kinds of pleasure in 1.8. The statement that Simonides makes in 2.1-2, is understood by Hiero in the light of Simonides' general statement, as appears from 2.3-5; 4.6; and 6.12. (Compare also 8.7 with 3.3). — For the interpretation of Simonides' initial question, consider Isocrates, *To Nicocles* 4-5.

[9] *Hiero* 2.3-5. One should also not forget the fact that the author of the *Hiero* never was a tyrant. — Compare Plato, *Republic* 577a-b and *Gorgias* 470d5-e11.

[10] *Memorabilia* I 3.2; IV 8.6; 5.9-10. Compare *Anabasis* VI 1.17-21.

[11] *Memorabilia* IV 6.1, 7; III 3.11; I 2.14.

[12] *Hiero* 1.21, 31.

[13] Compare *Hiero* 11.5-6 and *Agesilaus* 9.6-7 with Pindar, *Ol.* I and *Pyth.* I-III.

[14] *Hiero* 1.14. — The same rule of conduct was observed by Socrates. Compare the manner in which he behaved when talking to the "legislators" Critias and Charicles, with his open blame of the Thirty which he pronounced "somewhere," i.e., not in the presence of the tyrants, and which had to be "reported" to Critias and Charicles (*Memorabilia* I 2.32-38; observe the repetition of ἀπαγγελθέντος). — In Plato's *Protagoras* (345e-346b8) Socrates excuses Simonides for having praised tyrants under compulsion.

[15] *Hiero* 1.9-10, 16-17; 2.3-5.

[16] *Hiero* 1.10; 8.1.

[17] *Hiero* 2.3-5.

[18] While all men consider tyrants enviable, while the multitude is deceived by the outward splendor of tyrants, the multitude does not wish to be ruled by tyrants but rather by the just. Compare *Hiero* 2.3-5 with *ib.* 5.1 and 4.5. — Compare Plato, *Republic* 344b5-c1.

[19] Compare the end of the *Oeconomicus* with *ib.* 6.12 ff. See also *Memorabilia* II 6.22 ff.

[20] *Hiero* 5.1; 1.1.

[21] *Hiero* 6.5. Aristotle, *Politics* 1314a10-13.

[22] *Hiero* 4.2. See note 14 above.

[23] *Hiero* 5.1-2.

[24] Hiero mentions "contriving something bad and base" in 4.10, i.e., almost immediately before the crucial passage. Compare also 1.22-23.

[25] *Memorabilia* I 2.31; IV 2.33. *Symposium* 6.6. *Apologia Socratis* 20-21. *Cyropaedia* III 1.39. Compare Plato, *Apol. Socr.* 23d4-7 and 28a6-b1, as well as *Seventh Letter* 344c1-3.

[26] *Memorabilia* I 6.12-13.

[27] Compare *Oeconomicus* 6.12 ff. and 11.1 ff. with *Memorabilia* I 1.16 and IV 6.7. Compare Plato, *Republic* 489e3-490a3. The distinction between the two meanings of "gentleman" corresponds to the Platonic distinction between common or political virtue and genuine virtue.

[28] *Cyropaedia* I 1.1. *Memorabilia* I 2.56; 6.11-12. Compare *Memorabilia* IV 2.33 with *Symposium* 3.4. See Plato, *Seventh Letter* 333b3 ff. and 334a1-3 as well as *Gorgias* 468e6-9 and 469c3 (cf. 492d2-3); also *Republic* 493a6 ff.

[29] *Memorabilia* I 2.31 ff.; IV 4.3. *Symposium* 4.13. Compare Plato, *Apol. Socr.* 20e8-21a3 and 32c4-d8 as well as *Gorgias* 480e6 ff.; also *Protagoras* 329e2-330a2. Cf. note 14 above.

[30] *Hellenica* IV 4.6. Compare *Symposium* 3.4.

[31] Whereas Hiero asserts that the tyrant is unjust, he does not say that he is foolish. Whereas he asserts that the entourage of the tyrant consists of the unjust, the intemperate and the servile, he does not say that it consists of fools. Consider the lack of correspondence between the virtues mentioned in *Hiero* 5.1. and the vices mentioned in 5.2. Moreover, by proving that he is wiser than the wise Simonides, Hiero proves that the tyrant may be wise indeed.

[32] According to Xenophon's Socrates, he who possesses the specific knowledge required for ruling well, is *eo ipso* a ruler (*Memorabilia* III 9.10; 1.4). Hence he who possesses the tyrannical art, is *eo ipso* a tyrant. From Xenophon's point of view, Hiero's distrust of Simonides is an ironical reflection of the Socratic truth. It is ironical for the following reason: From Xenophon's point of view, the wise teacher of the royal art, or of the tyrannical art, is not a potential ruler in the ordinary sense of the term, because he who knows how to rule does not necessarily wish to rule. Even

Hiero grants by implication that the just do not wish to rule, or that they wish merely to mind their own business (cf. *Hiero* 5.1 with *Memorabilia* I 2.48 and II 9.1). If the wise man is necessarily just, the wise teacher of the tyrannical art will not wish to be a tyrant. But it is precisely the necessary connection between wisdom and justice which is questioned by Hiero's distinction between the wise and the just.

[33] *Hiero* 2.3-5 (compare the wording with that used *ib.* 1.9 and in *Cyropaedia* IV 2.28). It should be emphasized that in this important passage Hiero does not speak explicitly of wisdom. (His only explicit remark on wisdom occurs in the central passage, *viz.* in 5.1). Furthermore, Hiero silently qualifies what he says about happiness in 2.3-5, in a later passage (7.9-10) where he admits that bliss requires outward or visible signs.

[34] *Hiero* 2.6 ; 1.10.

[35] Hiero states at the beginning that Simonides is a wise *man* (ἀνήρ) ; but as Simonides expains in 7.3-4, (real) men (ἄνδρες) as distinguished from (ordinary) human beings (ἄνθρωποι) are swayed by ambition and hence apt to aspire to tyrannical power. (The ἀνδρός at the end of 1.1 corresponds to the ἀνθρώποις at the end of 1.2. Cf. also 7.9, beginning.) Shortly after the beginning, Hiero remarks that Simonides is "at present still a private man" (1.3), thus implying that he might well become a tyrant. Accordingly, Hiero speaks only once of "you (private men)," whereas Simonides speaks fairly frequently of "you (tyrants)": Hiero hesitates to consider Simonides as merely a private man. (6.10. The "you" in 2.5 refers to the reputedly wise men as distinguished from the multitude. Simonides speaks of "you tyrants" in the following passages: 1.14, 16, 24, 26 ; 2.2 ; 7.2, 4 ; 8.7). — For the distinction between "real men" and "ordinary human beings," compare also *Anabasis* I 7.4 ; *Cyropaedia* IV 2.25 ; V 5.33 ; Plato, *Republic* 550a1 ; *Protagoras* 316c5-317b5.

[36] *Hiero* 1.9 ; 6.2. ζηλόω, the term used by Simonides and later on by Hiero, designates jealousy, the noble counterpart of envy rather than envy proper (cf. Aristotle, *Rhetoric* II 11). That the tyrant is exposed to envy in the strict sense of the term, appears from Hiero's remark in 7.10 and from Simonides' emphatic promise at the end of the dialogue: the tyrant who has become the benefactor of his subjects will be happy without being envied. Cf. also 11.6 where it is implied that a tyrant like Hiero is envied (cf. note 13 above). In *Hiero* 1.9, Simonides avoids speaking of "envy" because the term might suggest that all men bear ill-will to the tyrant, and this implication would spoil completely the effect of his statement. Hiero's statement in 6.12, which refers not only to 1.9 but to 2.2 as well, amounts to a correction of what Simonides had said in the former passage ; Hiero suggests that not all men, but only men like Simonides are jealous of the tyrant's wealth and power. As for Simonides' distinction (in 1.9) between "all men" who are jealous of tyrants and the "many" who desire to be tyrants, it has to be understood as follows: many who consider a thing an enviable possession, do not seriously desire it, because they are convinced of their inability to acquire it. — Compare Aristotle, *Politics* 1311a29-31 and 1313a17-23.

[37] By using the tyrant's fear as a means for his betterment, Simonides acts in accordance with a pedagogic principle of Xenophon ; see *Hipparchicus* 1.8 ; *Memorabilia* III 5.5-6 ; *Cyropaedia* III 1.23-24.

[38] Compare *Hiero* 1.14 with 1.16. Note the emphatic character of Simonides' assent to Hiero's reply (1.16, beginning). Compare also 2.2 with 11.2-5.

[39] Compare *Hiero* 4.5 with *Hellenica* VI 4.32 and VII 3.4-6.

[40] Compare *Hiero* 6.14 with *Hellenica* VII 3.12.

⁴¹ Compare *Hiero* 6.1-3 with *Cyropaedia* I 3.10, 18.

⁴² Compare *Hiero* 8.6 with *ib.* 2.1. The statement is not contradicted by Hiero; it is prepared, and thus to a certain extent confirmed, by what Hiero says in 1.27 (Νῦν δή) and 1.29. In 7.5, Hiero indicates that agreement had been reached between him and Simonides on the subject of sex.

⁴³ *Hiero* 2.12-18.

⁴⁴ By showing this, Hiero elaborates what we may call the gentleman's image of the tyrant. Xenophon pays a great compliment to Hiero's education by entrusting to him the only elaborate presentation of the gentleman's view of tyranny which he ever wrote. Compare p. 10 above on the relation between the *Hiero* and the *Agesilaus*. — The relation of Hiero's indictment of tyranny to the true account of tyranny can be compared to the relation of the Athenian story about the family of Pisistratus to Thucydides' "exact" account. One may also compare it to the relation of the *Agesilaus* to the corresponding sections of the *Hellenica*.

⁴⁵ *Memorabilia* IV 4.10. *Agesilaus* 1.6. — As for the purpose of the *Hellenica*, compare IV 8.1 and V 1.4 with II 3.56 as well as with *Symposium* 1.1 and *Cyropaedia* VIII 7.24.

⁴⁶ *Memorabilia* I 2.58-61. While Xenophon denies the charge that Socrates had interpreted the verses in question in a particularly obnoxious manner, he does not deny the fact that Socrates frequently quoted the verses. Why Socrates liked them, or how he interpreted them, is indicated *ib.* IV 6. 13-15: Socrates used two types of dialectics, one which leads to the truth and another which, by never leaving the dimension of generally accepted opinions, leads to (political) agreement. For the interpretation of the passage, compare *Symposium* 4.59-60 with *ib.* 4.56-58.

⁴⁷ *Symposium* 3.6. Compare Plato, *Republic* 378d6-8 and a1-6.

⁴⁸ To summarize our argument, we shall say that if Hiero is supposed to state the truth or even merely to be completely frank, the whole *Hiero* becomes unintelligible. If one accepts either supposition, one will be compelled to agree with the following criticism by Ernst Richter ("Xenophon-Studien," *Fleckeisen's Jahrbücher für classische Philologie*, 19. Supplementband, 1893, 149) : "Einem solchen Manne, der sich so freimüthig über sich selbst äussert, und diese lobenswerten Gesinnungen hegt, möchte man kaum die Schreck-ensthaten zutrauen, die er als von der Tyrannenherrschaft unzertrennlich hinstellt. Hat er aber wirklich soviel Menschen getötet und übt er täglich noch soviel Übelthaten aus, ist für ihn wirklich das Beste der Strick—und er musste es ja wissen—, so kommen die Ermahnungen des Simonides im zweiten Teil ganz gewiss zu spät. . . . Simonides gibt Ratschläge, wie sie nur bei einem Fürsten vom Schlage des Kyros oder Agesilaos angebracht sind, nie aber bei einem Tyrannen, wie ihn Hieron beschreibt, der schon gar nicht mehr weiss, wie er sich vor seinen Todfeinden schützen kann." Not to repeat what we have said in the text, the quick transition from Hiero's indictment of the tyrant's injustice (7.7-13) to his remark that the tyrants punish the unjust (8.9) is unintelligible but for the fact that his account is exaggerated. If one supposes then that Hiero exaggerates, one has to wonder why he exaggerates. Now, Hiero himself makes the following assertions: that the tyrants trust no one; that they fear the wise; that Simonides is a real man; and that Simonides admires, or is jealous of, the tyrants' power. These assertions of Hiero supply us with the only authentic clue to the riddle of the dialogue. Some of the assertions referred to are without doubt as much suspect of being exaggerated as almost all other assertions of Hiero. But this very fact implies that they contain an element of truth, or that they are true if taken with a grain of salt.

b. The action

[1] *Hiero* 1.3. As for the duration of Hiero's reign, see Aristotle, *Politics* 1315b35 ff. and Diodorus Siculus XI 38. Hiero shows later on (*Hiero* 6.1-2) that he recalls very well certain pleasures of private men of which he had not been reminded by Simonides.

[2] *Hiero* 1.4-5. The "we" in "we all know" in 1.4 refers of course to private men and tyrants alike. Compare 1.29 and 10.4.

[3] *Hiero* 1.4-6. To begin with, i.e., before Simonides has aroused his opposition, Hiero does not find any difference between tyrants and private men in regard to sleep (1.7). Later on, in an entirely different conversational situation, Hiero takes up "the pleasures of private men of which the tyrant is deprived"; in that context, while elaborating the gentleman's image of the tyrant (with which Simonides must be presumed to have been familiar from the outset), Hiero speaks in the strongest terms of the difference between tyrants and private men in regard to the enjoyment of sleep (6.3,7-10).

[4] Twelve out of fifteen classes of pleasant or painful things are unambiguously of a bodily nature. The three remaining classes are 1) the good things, 2) the bad things and 3) sleep. As for the good and the bad things, Simonides says that they please or pain us sometimes through the working of the soul alone and sometimes through that of the soul and the body together. As regards sleep, he leaves open the question by means of what kind of organ or faculty we enjoy it.

[5] Compare *Hiero* 2.1 and 7.3 with *Memorabilia* II 1.

[6] *Hiero* 1.19. Compare Isocrates, *To Nicocles* 4.

[7] Compare *Hiero* 4.8-9 with *Memorabilia* IV 2.37-38.

[8] *Hiero* 1.7-10. Hiero's oath in 1.10 is the first oath occurring in the dialogue. Hiero uses the emphatic form μὰ τὸν Δία.

[9] See in *Hiero* 1.10 the explicit reference to the order of Simonides' enumeration.

[10] The proof is based on λογισμός, i.e., on a comparison of data that are supplied by experience or observation. Compare *Hiero* 1.11 (λογιζόμενος εὑρίσκω) with the reference to ἐμπειρία in 1.10. Compare *Memorabilia* IV 3.11 and *Hellenica* VIII 4.2.

[11] The passage consists of five parts: 1) "sights" (Hiero contributes 163 words, Simonides is silent); 2) "sounds" (Hiero 36 words, Simonides 68 words); 3) "food" (Hiero 230 words, Simonides 76 words); 4) "odors" (Hiero is silent, Simonides 32 words); 5) "sex" (Hiero 411 words, Simonides 42 words). Hiero is most vocal concerning "sex"; Simonides is most vocal concerning "food."

[12] Compare III a, note 42, and III b, notes 11 and 19. As for the connection between sexual love and tyranny, cf. Plato, *Republic* 573e6-7, 574e2 and 575a1-2.

[13] *Hiero* 1.31-33.

[14] Compare *Hiero* 1.16 with the parallels in 1.14, 24, 26.

[15] Simonides' first oath (μὰ τὸν Δία) occurs in the passage dealing with sounds, i.e., with praise (1.16).

[10] Rudolf Hirzel, *Der Dialog*, I, Leipzig, 1895, 171, notes "die geringe Lebendigkeit des Gesprächs, die vorherrschende Neigung zu längeren Vorträgen": all the more striking is the character of the discussion of "food."

[17] Simonides grants this by implication in *Hiero* 1.26.

[18] Mr. Marchant (Xenophon, *Scripta Minora, Loeb's Classical Library*, XV-XVI) says: "There is no attempt at characterization in the persons of the dialogue. . . . The remark of the poet at c.1.22 is singularly inappropriate

to a man who had a liking for good living." In the passage referred to, Simonides declares that "acid, pungent, astringent and kindred things" are "very unnatural for human beings": he says nothing at all against "sweet and kindred things." The view that bitter, acid, etc., things are "against nature," was shared by Plato (*Timaeus* 65c-66c), by Aristotle (*Eth. Nic.* 1153a5-6; cf. *De anima* 422b 10-14) and, it seems, by Alcmæon (cf. Aristotle, *Metaphysics* 986a22-34). Moreover, Simonides says that acid, pungent, etc. things are unnatural for "human beings"; but "human beings" may have to be understood in contradistinction to "real men" (cf. III a, note 35 above). At any rate, the fare censured by Simonides is recommended as a fare for soldiers by Cyrus in a speech addressed to "real men" (*Cyropaedia* VI 2.31). (Compare also *Symposium* 4.9.) Above all, Marchant who describes the *Hiero* as "a naive little work, not unattractive," somewhat naively overlooks the fact that Simonides' utterances serve primarily the purpose, not of characterizing Simonides, but of influencing Hiero; they characterize the poet in a more subtle way than the one which alone is considered by Marchant: the fact that Simonides indicates, or fails to indicate, his likes or dislikes according to the requirements of his pedagogic intentions, characterizes him as wise.

19 *Hiero* 1.26. "Sex" is the only motive of which Simonides ever explicitly says that it could be the only motive for desiring tyrannical power. Compare note 12 above.

20 *Hiero* 7.5-6.

21 *Hiero* 8.6.

22 Note the increased emphasis on "(real) men" in *Hiero* 2.1. In the parallel passage of the first section (1.9), Simonides had spoken of "most able (real) men." Compare the corresponding change of emphasis in Hiero's replies (see the following note).

23 Compare *Hiero* 1.16-17 with 2.1 where Simonides declares that the bodily pleasures appear to him to be very minor things and that, as he observes, many of those who are reputed to be real men do not attach any great value to those pleasures. Hiero's general statement in 2.3-5, which is so much stronger than his corresponding statement in the first section (1.10), amounts to a tacit rejection of Simonides' claim: Hiero states that the view expressed by Simonides in 2.1-2, far from being non-vulgar, is *the* vulgar view.

24 *Hiero* 2.1-2. Simonides does not explicitly speak of "wealth and power." "Wealth and power" had been mentioned by Hiero in 1.27. (Compare Aristotle, *Politics* 1311a8-12.) — On the basis of Simonides' initial enumeration (1.4-6) one would expect that the second section (ch. 2-6) would deal with the three kinds of pleasure that had not been discussed in the first section, *viz.* the objects perceived by the whole body, the good and bad things, and sleep. Only good and bad things and, to a lesser degree, sleep are clearly discernible as subjects of the second section. As for good and bad things, see the following passages: 2.6-7; 3.1, 3, 5; 4.1; 5.2, 4. (Compare also 2.2 with *Anabasis* III 1.19-20.) As for sleep, see 6.3-9. As for objects perceived by the whole body, compare 1.5 and 2.2 with *Memorabilia* III 8.8-9 and 10.13. Sleep (the last item of the initial enumeration) is not yet mentioned in the retrospective summary at the beginning of the second section, whereas it is mentioned in the parallel at the beginning of the third section (cf. 2.1 with 7.3); in this manner Xenophon indicates that the discussion of the subjects mentioned in the inital enumeration is completed at the end of the second section: the third section deals with an entirely new subject.

25 Simonides merely intimates it, for he does not say in so many words

that "they aspire to greater things, to power and wealth." Taken by itself, the statement with which Simonides opens the second section is much less far-reaching than the statements with which he had opened the discussion of the first section (1.8-9, 16). But one has to understand the later statement in the light of the earlier ones, if one wants to understand the conversational situation. Compare III a, note 8 above.

26 Simonides fails to mention above all the field or farm which occupies the central position among the objects desired by private men (*Hiero* 4.7) and whose cultivation is praised by Socrates as a particularly pleasant possession (*Oeconomicus* 5.11). Compare also *Hiero* 11.1-4 with *ib.* 4.7 and *Memorabilia* III 11.4. Simonides pushes into the background the pleasures of private men who limit themselves to minding their own business instead of being swayed by political ambition (see *Memorabilia* I 2.48 and II 9.1). Farming is a skill of peace (*Oeconomicus* 4.12 and 1.17). Simonides also fails to mention dogs (compare *Hiero* 2.2 with *Agesilaus* 9.6). — Compare *De vectigalibus* 4.8.

27 Whereas we find in the first section an explicit reference to the order of Simonides' enumeration (1.10), no such reference occurs in the second section. In the second section Hiero refers only once explicitly to the statement with which Simonides had opened the section, i.e., to 2.1-2; he does this, however, only after (and in fact almost immediately after) Simonides has made his only contribution to the discussion of the second section (6.12-13). An obvious, although implicit, reference to 2.2 occurs in 4.6-7. (Cf. especially the θᾶττον. . . . . . κατεργάζεσθαι in 4.7 with the ταχὺ κατεργάζεσθε in 2.2). The αὐτίκα in 2.7 (peace-war) refers to the last item mentioned in 2.2 (enemies-friends). These references merely underline the deviation of Hiero's speech from Simonides' enumeration. — Simonides' silence is emphasized by Xenophon's repeated mention of the fact that Simonides has been listening to Hiero's speeches, i.e., that Simonides had not spoken (see 6.9; 7.1, 11). There is no mention of Hiero's listening to Simonides' statements.

28 See note 25 above.

29 As for Simonides, see pp. 12-13 above. Hiero's concern with wealth is indicated by the fact that, deviating from Simonides, he explicitly mentions the receiving of gifts among the signs of honor (compare 7.7-9 with 7.2). To comply with Hiero's desire, Simonides promises him later on (11.12) gifts among other things. Compare Aristotle, *Politics* 1311a8 ff. and note 74 below. Consider also the emphatic use of "possession" in Simonides' final promise.— Simonides' silence about love of gain as distinguished from love of honor (compare *Hiero* 7.1-4 with *Oeconomicus* 14.9-10) is remarkable. It appears from *Hiero* 9.11 and 11.12-13 that the same measures which would render the tyrant honored, would render him rich as well.

30 Friendship as discussed by Hiero in ch. 3 is something different from "helping friends" which is mentioned by Simonides in 2.2. The latter topic is discussed by Hiero in 6.12-13.

31 Compare 2.8 with 1.11-12; 3.7-9 with 1.38; 3.8 and 4.1-2 with 1.27-29; 4.2 with 1.17-25. In the cited passages of ch. 1, as distinguished from the parallels in ch. 2 ff., no mention of "killing of tyrants" occurs. Compare also the insistence on the moral depravity of the tyrant, or on his injustice, in the second section (5.1-2 and 4.11) with the only mention of "injustice" in the first section (1.12): in the first section only the "injustice" *suffered* by tyrants is mentioned. As regards 1.36, see note 41 below.

32 Marchant (*loc. cit.*, XVI) remarks that Xenophon "makes no attempt anywhere to represent the courtier poet; had he done so he must have made Simonides bring in the subject of verse panegyrics on princes at

c. I.14." It is hard to judge of this suggested improvement on the *Hiero*
since Marchant does not tell us how far the remark on verse panegyrics on
princes would have been more conducive than what Xenophon's Simonides
actually says, towards the achievement of Simonides' aim. Besides, compare
Hiero 9.4 with 9.2. — We read in Macaulay's essay on Frederick the Great:
"Nothing can be conceived more whimsical than the conferences which took
place between the first literary man and the first practical man of the age,
whom a strange weakness had induced to exchange their parts. The great
poet would talk of nothing but treaties and guarantees, and the great king
of nothing but metaphors and rhymes."

³³ *Hiero* 3.6 ; 4.6 ; 5.1.

³⁴ Note the frequent use of the second person singular in ch. 3, and the
ascent from the καταθέασαι in 3.1 to the εἰ βούλει εἰδέναι, ἐπίσκεψαι
in 3.6 and finally to the εἰ τοίνυν ἐθέλεις κατανοεῖν in 3.8.

³⁵ *Hiero* 6.1-6.

³⁶ Compare *Hiero* 6.7 with *ib.* 6.3.

³⁷ *Hiero* 6.7-9. — The importance of Simonides' remark is underlined by
the following three features of Hiero's reply: First, that reply opens with
the only oath that occurs in the second section. Second, that reply, being
one of the three passages of the *Hiero* in which laws are mentioned (3.9 ; 4.4 ;
6.10), is the only passage in the dialogue in which it is clearly intimated
that tyrannical government is government without laws, i.e., it is the only
passage in Xenophon's only work on tyranny in which the essential character
of tyranny comes, more or less, to light. Third, Hiero's reply is the only
passage of the *Hiero* in which Hiero speaks of "you (private men)" (see
III a, note 35 above). Compare also III b, note 27 above.

³⁸ The character of Simonides' only contribution to the discussion of
the second section can also be described as follows: While he was silent
when friendship was being discussed, he talks in a context in which war
is mentioned ; he is more vocal regarding war than regarding friendship.
See note 26 above.

³⁹ The situation is illustrated by the following figures: In the first section
(1.10-38) Simonides contributes about 218 words out of about 1058 ; in the
second section (2.3-6.16) he contributes 28 words out of about 2,000 ; in the
third section (ch. 7) he contributes 220 words out of 522 ; in the fourth
section (ch. 8-11) he contributes about 1,475 words out of about 1,600.—
K. Lincke, "Xenophon's Hiero und Demetrios von Phaleron," *Philologus*, v.
58, 1899, 226, correctly describes the "Sinnesänderung" of Hiero as "die
Peripetie des Dialogs."

⁴⁰ Compare note 24 above. The initial enumeration had dealt explicitly
with the pleasures of "human beings" (see III a, note 35 above), but honor,
the subject of the third section, is the aim, not of "human beings," but of
"real men." One has no right to assume that the subject of the third section
is the pleasures or pains of the soul, and the subject of the second section
is the pleasures or pains common to body and soul. In the first place, the
pleasures or pains of the soul precede in the initial enumeration the pleasures or pains common to body and soul ; besides, ἐπινοεῖν, which is mentioned in the enumeration that opens the second section (2.2), is certainly
an activity of the soul alone ; finally, the relation of honor to praise as well
as the examples adduced by Simonides show clearly that the pleasure connected with honor is not meant to be a pleasure of the soul alone (compare
7.2-3 with 1.14). When Simonides says that no human pleasure comes nearer
to the divine than the pleasure concerning honors, he does not imply that
that pleasure is a pleasure of the soul alone, for, apart from other considerations, it is an open question whether Simonides, or Xenophon, considered

the deity an incorporeal being. As for Xenophon's view on this subject, compare *Memorabilia* I 4.17 and context (for the interpretation consider Cicero, *De natura deorum* I 12.30-31 and III 10.26-27) as well as *ib.* IV 3.13-14. Compare *Cynegeticus* 12.19 ff.

41 Compare *Hiero* 7.1-4 with *ib.* 2.1-2. See III a, note 8, and III b, note 22 above. — The "many" (in the expression "for many of those who are reputed to be real men") is emphasized by the insertion of "he said" after "for many" (2.1), and the purpose of this emphasis is to draw our attention to the still limited character of the thesis that opens the second section. This is not the only case in which Xenophon employs this simple device for directing the reader's attention. The "he said" after "we seem" in 1.5 draws our attention to the fact that Simonides uses here for the first time the first person when speaking of private men. The two redundant "he said"'s in 1.7-8 emphasize the "he answered" which precedes the first of these two two "he said"'s, thus making it clear that Simonides' preceding enumeration of pleasures has the character of a question addressed to Hiero, or that Simonides is testing Hiero. The second "he said" in 1.31 draws our attention to the preceding σύ, i.e., to the fact that Hiero's assertion concerning tyrants in general is now applied by Simonides to Hiero in particular. The "he said" in 1.36 draws our attention to the fact that the tyrant Hiero hates to behave like a brigand. The redundant "he said" in 7.1 draws our attention to the fact that the following praise of honor is based on εἰκότα. The "he said" in 7.13 emphasizes the preceding ἴσθι, i.e., the fact that Hiero does not use in this context the normally used εὖ ἴσθι, for he is now describing in the strongest possible terms how bad tyranny is.

42 *Hiero* 7.5-10.

43 Compare *Hiero* 7.3 with *ib.* 1.14-15.

44 In the third section, Simonides completely abandons the vulgar opinion in favor, not of the gentleman's opinion, but of the opinion of the real man. The aim of the real man is distinguished from that of the gentleman by the fact that honor as striven for by the former does not essentially presuppose a just life. Compare *Hiero* 7.3 with *Oeconomicus* 14.9.

45 *Hiero* 7.11-13. I have put in brackets the thoughts which Hiero does not express. As for Simonides' question, compare *Anabasis* VII 7.28.

46 *Hiero* 1.12. As for the tyrant's fear of punishment, see *ib.* 5.2.

47 Regarding strangers, see *Hiero* 1.27; 5.3; 6.5.

48 Compare *Hiero* 8.9 with *ib.* 7.7 and 5.2.

49 Simonides continues asserting that tyrannical life is superior to private life; compare *Hiero* 8.1-7 with *ib.* 1.8 ff.; 2.1-2; 7.1 ff.

50 *Hiero* 7.12-13.

51 When comparing *Hiero* 7.13 with *Apologia Socratis* 7 and 32, one is led to wonder why Hiero is contemplating such an unpleasant form of death as hanging: does he belong to those who never gave thought to the question of the easiest way of dying? Or does he thus reveal that he never seriously considered committing suicide? Compare also *Anabasis* II 6.29.

52 *Memorabilia* I 2.10-11, 14.

53 "You are out of heart with tyranny because you believe. . . ." (*Hiero* 8.1).

54 Compare also the transition from "tyranny" to the more general "rule" in *Hiero* 8.1 ff. Regarding the relation of "tyranny" and "rule," see *Memorabilia* IV 6.12; Plato, *Republic* 338d7-11; Aristotle, *Politics* 1276a2-4.

55 *Hiero* 7.5-6, 9; compare *ib.* 1.37-38 and 3.8-9.

56 *Hiero* 8.1.

57 *Hiero* 8.1-7. Compare note 54 above.

58 Compare *Hiero* 1.36-38.

⁵⁹ In this context (8.3), there occur allusions. to the topics discussed in 1.10 ff: ἰδών (sights), ἐπαινεσάντων (sounds), θύσας (food). The purpose of this is to indicate the fact that Simonides is now discussing the subject matter of the first part from the opposite point of view.

⁶⁰ *Memorabilia* II 1.27-28; 3.10-14; 6.10-16. Compare *Anabasis* I 9. 20 ff.

⁶¹ If Simonides had acted differently, he would have appeared as a just man, and Hiero would fear him. Whereas Hiero's fear of the just is definite, his fear of the wise is indeterminate (see pp. 21-25 above); it may prove to be unfounded in a given case. This is what actually happens in the *Hiero*: Simonides convinces Hiero that the wise can be friends of tyrants. — One cannot help being struck by the contrast between Simonides' "censure" of the tyrant Hiero and the prophet Nathan's accusation of the Lord's anointed King David (II Samuel 12).

⁶² *Hiero* 8.8. The equally unique πάλιν (εἶπεν) in 9.1 draws our attention to the εὐθύς in 8.8.

⁶³ *Hiero* 8.8-10. Compare *ib.* 6.12-13.

⁶⁴ *Hiero* 9.1. Observe the negative formulation of Simonides' assent to a statement dealing with unpleasant aspects of tyrannical rule.

⁶⁵ Simonides' speech consists of two parts. In the fairly short first part (9.1-4), he states the general principle. In the more extensive second part (9.5-11), he makes specific proposals regarding its application by the tyrant. In the second part punishment and the like are no longer mentioned. The unpleasant aspects of tyranny, or of government in general, are also barely alluded to in the subsequent chapters. Probably the most charming expression of the poet's dignified silence about these disturbing things occurs in 10.8. There, Simonides refrains from mentioning the possibility that the tyrant's mercenaries, these angels of mercy, might actually punish the evildoers: he merely mentions how they should behave towards the innocent, towards those who intend to do evil and towards the injured. Compare the preceding note. — Compare also the statement of the Athenian stranger in Plato's *Laws* 711b4-c2 with the subsequent statement of Clinias.

⁶⁶ As for bewitching tricks to be used by absolute rulers, see *Cyropaedia* VIII 1.40-42; 2.26; 3.1. These less reserved remarks are those of a historian or a spectator rather than of an adviser. Compare Aristotle, *Politics* 1314a40: the tyrant ought to *play* the king.

⁶⁷ Ch. 9 and ch. 10 are the only parts of the *Hiero* in which "tyrant" and derivatives are avoided.

⁶⁸ Compare especially *Hiero* 9.10 with *ib.* 11.10.

⁶⁹ *Hiero* 9.7, 11.

⁷⁰ *Hiero* 9.6. Compare Aristotle, *Politics* 1315a31-40.

⁷¹ *Hiero* 8.10.

⁷² *Hiero* 10.1.

⁷³ *Hiero* 10.2. Compare Aristotle, *Politics* 1314a33 ff.

⁷⁴ Compare *Hiero* 4.9, 11 with 4.3 ("without pay") and 10.8.

⁷⁵ Compare *Hiero* 11.1 with 9.7-11 and 10.8.

⁷⁶ *Hiero* 11.1-6. Compare p. 18 above. — One is tempted to suggest that the *Hiero* represents Xenophon's interpretation of the contest between Simonides and Pindar.

⁷⁷ *Hiero* 11.7-15. Compare Plato, *Republic* 465d2-e2.

⁷⁸ K. Lincke (*loc. cit.*, 244), however, feels "dass Hiero eines Besseren belehrt worden wäre, muss der Leser sich hinzudenken, obgleich es . . . besser wäre, wenn man die Zustimmung ausgesprochen sähe." The Platonic parallel to Hiero's silence at the end of the *Hiero* is Callicles' silence at the end of the *Gorgias* and Thrasymachus' silence in books II-X of the *Republic*.

c. The use of characteristic terms

[1] Marchant, *loc. cit.*, XVI.

[2] For instance, Nabis is called "principe" in *Principe* IX and "tiranno" in *Discorsi* I 40, and Pandolfo Petruzzi is called "principe" in *Principe* XX and XXII, and "tiranno" in *Discorsi* III 6. Compare also the transition from "tyrant" to "ruler" in the second part of the *Hiero*.

[3] Compare *Hellenica* VI 3.8, end.

[4] *Hiero* 9.6.

[5] *Hiero* 11.6; 1.31. Compare *Apologia Socratis* 28, a remark which Socrates made "laughingly."

[6] Compare the absence of courage (or manliness) from the lists of Socrates' virtues: *Memorabilia* IV 8.11 (cf. IV 4.1 ff.) and *Apologia Socratis* 14, 16. Compare *Symposium* 9.1 with *Hiero* 7.3. But consider also II, note 22 above.

[7] Compare *Hiero* 9.8 on the one hand with 1.8, 19 and 5.1-2 on the other

[8] *Hiero* 10.1.

IV. THE TEACHING CONCERNING TYRANNY

[1] Aristotle, *Politics* 1313a33-38.

[2] This explanation does not contradict the one suggested on pp. 12-13 above, for the difference between a wise man who does not care to discover, or to teach, the tyrannical art, and a wise man who does, remains important and requires an explanation.

[3] *Hiero* 1.9-10; 2.3, 5.

[4] Compare *Hiero* 5.2 with the situations in *Cyropaedia* VII 2.10 on the one hand, and *ib.* VII 5.47 on the other.

[5] *Memorabilia* IV 6.12. Compare *Cyropaedia* I 3.18 and 1.1; *Hellenica* VII 1.46; *Agesilaus* 1.4; *De vectigalibus* 3.11; Aristotle, *Politics* 1295a15-18.

[6] *Hiero* 11.12. Compare *Hellenica* V 1.3-4.

[7] Compare pp. 47-48 and III b, note 37 above. In *Hiero* 7.2 Simonides says that *all* subjects of tyrants execute *every* command of the tyrant. Compare his additional remark that all rise from their seats in honor of the tyrant with *Resp. Lac.* 15.6: no ephors limit the tyrant's power. — According to Rousseau (*Contrat social* III 10) the *Hiero* confirms his thesis that the Greeks understood by a tyrant not, as Aristotle in particular did, a bad monarch but a usurper of royal authority regardless of the quality of his rule. According to the *Hiero*, the tyrant is necessarily "lawless" not merely because of the manner in which he acquired his position, but above all because of the manner in which he rules: he follows his own will which may be good or bad, and not any law. Xenophon's "tyrant" is identical with Rousseau's "despot" (*Contrat social* III 10 end). Compare Montesquieu, *De l'esprit des lois* XI 9 and XIV 13 note.

[8] *Hiero* 11.8, 15. Compare *ib.* 8.9 with 7.10-12, 7 and 11.1. Compare also 1.11-14 with the parallel in the *Memorabilia* (II 1.31). Regarding the fact that the tyrant may be just, compare Plato, *Phaedrus* 248e3-5.

[9] *Hiero* 11.5, 7, 14-15.

[10] *Hiero* 8.3 and 9.2-10.

[11] *Hiero* 9.6 and 11.3, 12. Compare *Hellenica* II 3.41; also Aristotle, *Politics* 1315a32-40 and Machiavelli, *Principe* XX.

[12] *Hiero* 10.6. Compare *Hellenica* IV 4.14.

[13] As regards prizes, compare especially *Hiero* 9.11 with *Hipparchicus* 1.26. Ernst Richter (*loc. cit.*, 107) goes so far as to say that "die Forderungen des zweiten (Teils des *Hiero*) genau die des Sokrates (sind)."

[14] *Hiero* 11.14; compare *ib.* 6.3 and 3.8.

[15] Compare *Cyropaedia* VIII 1.1 and 8.1.

16 Compare *Hiero* 10.4 with *ib.* 4.3.

17 *Hiero* 9.1 ff. Compare Machiavelli, *Principe* XIX and XXI, towards the end as well as Aristotle, *Politics* 1315a4-8. See also Montesquieu, *De l'esprit des lois* XII 23-24. — As for the reference to the division of the city into sections in Hiero 9.5-6 (cf. Machiavelli, *Principe* XXI, towards the end), one might compare Aristotle, *Politics* 1305a30-34 and Hume's "Idea of a perfect commonwealth" (towards the end).

18 *Memorabilia* III 4.8, *Oeconomicus* 4.7-8; 9.14-15; 12.19. *Resp. Lac.* 4.6 and 8.4. *Cyropaedia* V 1.13. *Aanabasis* V 8.18 and II 6.19-20. Compare, however, *Cyropaedia* VIII 1.18.

19 Compare *Hiero* 9.7-8 with *Resp. Lac.* 7.1-2. Compare Aristotle, *Politics* 1305a18-22 and 1313b18-28 as well as Montesquieu, *De l'esprit des lois* XIV 9.

20 *Hiero* 11.12-14. Compare *Cyropaedia* VIII 2.15, 19; 1.17 ff.

21 Compare *Hiero* 8.10 and 11.13 with *Oeconomicus* 14.9.

22 *Hiero* 1.16.

23 Plato, *Republic* 562b9-c3; *Euthydemus* 292b4-c1. Aristotle, *Eth. Nic.* 1131a26-29 and 1161a6-9; *Politics* 1294a10-13; *Rhetoric* 1365b29 ff.

24 Compare p. 23 above.

25 *Hiero* 7.9 and 11.8. Compare *ib.* 2.2 (horses), 6.15 (horses) and 11.5 (chariots). The horse is the example used for the indirect characterization of political virtue in the *Oeconomicus* (11.3-6): a horse can possess virtue without possessing wealth; whether a human being can possess virtue without possessing wealth, remains there an open question. The political answer to the question is given in the *Cyropaedia* (I 2.15) where it is shown that aristocracy is the rule of well-bred men of independent means. — Compare pp. 54-55 above about the insecurity of property rights under a tyrant.

26 *Resp. Lac.* 10.4 (cf. Aristotle, *Eth. Nic.* 1180a24 ff.). *Cyropaedia* I 2.2 ff.

27 *Hiero* 9.6.

28 *Hiero* 5.1-2.

29 Compare *Hiero* 9.6 with *ib.* 5.3-4, *Anabasis* IV 3.4 and *Hellenica* VI 1.12. Compare *Hiero* 9.6 with the parallel in the *Cyropaedia* (I 2.12). A reduced form of prowess might seem to be characteristic of eunuchs; see *Cyropaedia* VII 5.61 ff.

30 This is the kind of justice that might exist in a non-political society like Plato's first city or city of pigs (*Republic* 371e12-372a4). Compare *Oeconomicus* 14.3-4 with Aristotle, *Eth. Nic.* 1130b6, 30 ff.

31 *Memorabilia* IV 8.11. *Apol. Socr.* 14, 16.

32 Compare *Hiero* 9.8 with *Memorabilia* IV 3.1 and *Hellenica* VII 3.6. Compare Plato, *Gorgias* 507a7-c3.

33 *Anabasis* VII 7.41.

34 *Hiero* 10.3. Compare Montesquieu, *De l'esprit des lois* III 9: "Comme il faut de la vertu dans une république, et dans une monarchie de l'honneur, il faut de la crainte dans un gouvernement despotique: pour la vertu, elle n'y est pas *nécessaire,* et l'honneur y serait *dangereux.*" Virtue is then not dangerous to "despotism." (The italics are mine.)

35 Compare *Hiero* 10.3 with *Cyropaedia* III 1.16 ff. and VIII 4.14 as well as with *Anabasis* VII 7.30.

36 *Anabasis* I 9.29.

37 Compare *Hiero* 11.5, 8 with *Memorabilia* III 2 and *Resp. Lac.* 1.2.

38 *Memorabilia* IV 4.12 ff. Compare *ib.* IV 6.5-6 and *Cyropaedia* I 3.17.

39 Aristotle, *Eth. Nic.* 1129b12.

40 *Memorabilia* IV 4.13.

[41] *Oeconomicus* 14.6-7.

[42] *Memorabilia* I 2.39-47 and I 1.16.

[43] *Memorabilia* I 2.31 ff.; IV 4.3.

[44] *Agesilaus* 4.2. Compare *Cyropaedia* I 2.7.

[45] Compare *Memorabilia* IV 8.11 with *ib.* I 2.7 and *Apol. Socr.* 26. See also *Agesilaus* 11.8. Compare Plato, *Crito* 49b10 ff. (cf. Burnet *ad loc.*) ; *Republic* 335d11-13 and 486b10-12 ; *Clitopho* 410a7-b3 ; Aristotle, *Politics* 1255a17-18 and *Rhetoric* 1367b5-6.

[46] *Cyropaedia* VIII 1.22.—In *Hiero* 9.9-10 Simonides recommends honors for those who discover something useful for the city. There is a connection between this suggestion which entails the acceptance of many and frequent changes, and the nature of tyrannical government as government not limited by laws. When Aristotle discusses the same suggestion which had been made by Hippodamus, he rejects it as dangerous to political stability and he is quite naturally led to state the principle that the "rule of law" requires as infrequent changes of laws as possible (*Politics,* 1268a6-8, b 22 ff.). The rule of laws as the classics understood it, can exist only in a "conservative" society. On the other hand, the speedy introduction of improvements of all kinds is obviously compatible with beneficent tyranny.

[47] *Hiero* 11.10-11. *Memorabilia* III 9.10-13. Compare Aristotle, *Politics* 1313a9-10. — It may be useful to compare the thesis of Xenophon with the thesis of such a convinced constitutionalist as Burke. Burke says (in his "Speech on a motion for leave to bring in a bill to repeal and alter certain acts respecting religious opinions") : ". . . it is not perhaps so much by the assumption of unlawful powers, as by the unwise or unwarrantable use of those which are most legal, that governments oppose their true end and object, for there is such a thing as tyranny as well as usurpation."

[48] *Cyropaedia* I 3.18.

[49] Compare *Anabasis* III 2.13. — Incidentally, the fact mentioned in the text accounts for the way in which tyranny is treated in Xenophon's emphatically Greek work, the *Hellenica.*

[50] *Memorabilia* III 9.12-13. Compare Plato, *Laws* 710c5-d1. — We are now in a position to state more clearly than we could at the beginning (pp. 10-11 above) the conclusion to be drawn from the title of the *Hiero.* The title expresses the view that Hiero is a man of eminence (cf. III a, note 44 above) but of questionable eminence ; that the questionable character of his eminence is revealed by the fact that he is in need of a teacher of the tyrannical art ; and that this is due, not only to his particular shortcomings, but to the nature of tyranny as such. The tyrant needs essentially a teacher, whereas the king (Agesilaus and Cyrus, e.g.) does not. We need not insist on the reverse side of this fact, *viz.,* that the tyrant rather than the king has any use for the wise man or the philosopher (consider the relation between Cyrus and the Armenian counterpart of Socrates in the *Cyropaedia*). If the social fabric is in order, if the régime is legitimate according to the generally accepted standards of legitimacy, the need for, and perhaps even the legitimacy of, philosophy is less evident than in the opposite case. Compare note 46 above and V, note 60 below.

[51] For an example of such transformations, compare *Cyropaedia* I 3.18 with *ib.* I 2.1.

[52] *Hiero* 10.1-8. Compare Aristotle, *Politics* 1311a7-8 and 1314a34 ff

[53] Aristotle, *Politics* 1276b29-36 ; 1278b1-5 ; 1293b3-7.

[54] *Memorabilia* I 2.9-11.

[55] Compare pp. 39-40 above.

[56] *Memorabilia* II 1.13-15.

[57] Compare also the qualified praise of the good tyrant by the Athenian stranger in Plato's *Laws* (709d10 ff. and 735d). In 709d10 ff. the Athenian stranger declines responsibility for the recommendation of the use of a tyrant by emphatically ascribing that recommendation to "the legislator."

V. THE TWO WAYS OF LIFE

[1] *Memorabilia* I 1.8; IV 6.14.

[2] Compare *Hiero* 1.2, 7 with *Cyropaedia* II 3.11 and VIII 3.35-48; *Memorabilia* II 1 and I 2.15-16; also Plato, *Gorgias* 500c-d.

[3] Consider the twofold meaning of ἰδιώτης in *Hiero* 4.6. Compare Aristotle, *Politics* 1266a31-32. — Whereas Hiero often uses "the tyrants" and "we" promiscuously, and Simonides often uses "the tyrants" and "you" promiscuously, Hiero makes only once a promiscuous use of "private men" and "you." Simonides speaks unambiguously of "we (private men)" in *Hiero* 1.5, 6 and in 6.9. For other uses of the first person plural by Simonides see the following passages: 1.4, 6, 16; 8.2, 5; 9.4; 10.4; 11.2. Compare III a, note 35 and III b, notes 2 and 41 above.

[4] Rudolf Hirzel, *loc. cit.*, 170 n. 3: "Am Ende klingt aus allen diesen (im Umlauf befindlichen) Erzählungen (über Gespräche zwischen Weisen und Herrschern) . . . dasselbe Thema wieder von dem *Gegensatz,* der zwischen den Mächtigen der Erde und den Weisen besteht und in deren gesamter Lebensauffassung und Anschauungsweise zu Tage tritt." (Italics mine.)

[5] *Hiero* 5.1. See p. 14 and III a, note 44 above.

[6] Plato, *Gorgias* 500c-d. Aristotle, *Politics* 1324a24 ff.

[7] Compare *Hiero* 9.2 with *Memorabilia* III 9.5, 10-11. Compare III a, note 32 above.

[8] *Memorabilia* I 2.16, 39, 47-48; 6.15; II 9.1; III 11.16.

[9] *Hiero* 7.13.

[10] Compare *Hiero* 8.1-10.1 with *ib.* 3.3-5 and 11.8-12.

[11] *Hiero* 7.4. Compare *ib.* 1.8-9 with 1.14, 16, 21-22, 24, 26 and 2.1-2.

[12] The difference between Simonides' explicit statements and Hiero's interpretation of them appears most clearly from a comparison of *Hiero* 2.1-2 with the following passages: 2.3-5; 4.6; 6.12.

[13] See pp. 19 and 33 and III b, notes 39 and 44 above.—In the second part (i.e., the fourth section) to which he contributes about three times as much as to the first part, Simonides uses expressions like "it seems to me" or "I believe" much less frequently than in the first part, while he uses in the second part three times ἐγὼ φημί which he never uses in the first part.

[14] *Hiero* 7.2,4. The ambiguity of διαφερόντως in 7.4 ("above other men" or "differently from other men") is not accidental. Compare with διαφερόντως in 7.4 the πολὺ διαφέρετε in 2.2, the πολὺ διαφερόντως in 1.29 and the πολλαπλάσια in 1.8. — Compare III a, note 8 and III b, notes 25 and 40 above.

[15] *Hiero* 8.1-7. Compare III b, note 38 above.

[16] *Hiero* 7.3-4.

[17] See pp. 45-46 and 48-49 above. Regarding the connection between "honor" and "noble," see *Cyropaedia* VII 1.13; *Memorabilia* III 1.1; 3.13; 5.28; *Oeconomicus* 21.6; *Resp. Lac.* 4.3-4; *Hipparchicus* 2.2.

[18] *Memorabilia* II 7.7-14 and III 9.14-15. *Cyropaedia* VIII 3.40 ff.

[19] *Hiero* 11.10; 1.13; 6.13. Compare *Cyropaedia* VII 2.26-29.

[20] In *Hiero* 11.15, the only passage in which Simonides applies "happy" and "blessed" to individuals, he does not explain the meaning of these terms. In the two passages in which he speaks of the happiness of the city, he understands by happiness power, wealth and renown (11.5, 7. Cf. *Resp. Lac.* 1.1-2). Accordingly, one could expect that he understands by the most noble

and most blessed possession that possession of power, wealth and renown which is not marred by envy. This expectation is, to say the least, not disproved by 11.13-15. Compare also *Cyropaedia* VIII 7.6-7; *Memorabilia* IV 2.34-35; *Oeconomicus* 4.23-5.1; *Hellenica* IV 1.36.

21 It is Hiero who on a certain occasion alludes to this meaning of "happiness" (2.3-5). Compare III a, note 33 above.

22 *Memorabilia* IV 8.11; I 6.14. Compare p. 22 and III a, note 25 above.

23 As for the danger of envy, see *Hiero* 11.6 and 7.10. As for the work and toil of the ruler, see 11.15 (ταῦτα πάντα) and 7.1-2. — Compare *Memorabilia* II 1.10.

24 *De vectigalibus* 4.5; *Resp. Lac.* 15.8; *Symposium* 3.9 and 4.2-3; *Anabasis* V 7.10. Compare also *Cyropaedia* I 6.24 and p. 45 above.

25 *Memorabilia* III 9.8; *Cynegeticus* 1.17. Compare Socrates' statements in the *Memorabilia* (IV 2.33) and the *Apol. Socr.* (26) with Xenophon's own statement in the *Cynegeticus* (1.11).

26 Compare note 23 above. Compare *Memorabilia* III 11.16; *Oeconomicus* 7.1 and 11.9; *Symposium* 4.44.

27 *Memorabilia* I 2.6; 5.6; 6.5; II 6.28-29; IV 1.2. *Symposium* 8.41. Compare *Memorabilia* IV 2.2 and *Cyropaedia* I 6.46. Consider the fact that the second part of the *Hiero* is characterized by the fairly frequent occurrence, not only of χάρις, but of ἀνάγκη as well (see p. 49 above).

28 *Memorabilia* IV 5.2; *Cyropaedia* I 5.12; *Anabasis* VII 7.41-42; *Symposium* 4.44.

29 *Memorabilia* II 4.5, 7; *Oeconomicus* 5.11. Compare III b, note 26 above.

30 As for the agreement between Simonides' final statement and the views expressed by Socrates and Xenophon, compare *Hiero* 11.5 with *Memorabilia* III 9.14, and *Hiero* 11.7 with *Agesilaus* 9.7.

31 Compare *Oeconomicus* 1.7 ff. with *Cyropaedia* I 3.17. Compare Isocrates, *To Demonicus* 28.

32 *Memorabilia* IV 5.6 and *Apol. Socr.* 21. Compare *Memorabilia* II 2.3; 4.2; I 2.7. As regards the depreciating remark on wisdom in *Memorabilia* IV 2.33, one has to consider the specific purpose of the whole chapter as indicated at its beginning. Ruling over willing subjects is called an almost divine good, not by Socrates but by Ischomachus (*Oeconomicus* 21.11-12).

33 *Memorabilia* I 4 and 6.10; IV 2.1 and 6.7. — Regarding the distinction between education and wisdom, see also Plato, *Laws* 653a5-c4 and 659c9 ff., and Aristotle, *Politics* 1282a3-8. Compare also *Memorabilia* II 1.27 where the παιδεία of Heracles is presented as preceding his deliberate choice between virtue and vice.

34 Compare *Hiero* 3.2 (and 6.1-3) with the parallel in the *Symposium* (8.18).

35 *Hiero* 9.1-11. Simonides does not explain what the best things are. From 9.4 it appears that according to Xenophon's Simonides the things which are taught by the teachers of choruses do not belong to the best things: the instruction given by the teachers of choruses is not gratifying to the pupils, and instructions in the best things is gratifying to the pupils. Following Simonides we shall leave it open whether the subjects mentoined in 9.6 (military discipline, horsemanship, justice in business dealings, etc.) meet the minimum requirements demanded of the best things, *viz.*, that instruction in them is gratifying to the pupils. The fact that he who executes these things well is honored by prizes, does not prove that they belong to the best things (cf. 9.4 and *Cyropaedia* III 3.33). Whether the things Simonides teaches are the best things will depend on whether the instruc-

tion that he gives to the tyrant is gratifying to the latter. The answer to this question remains as ambiguous as Hiero's silence at the end of the dialogue. — Xenophon uses in the *Hiero* the terms εὖ εἰδέναι and εὖ ποιεῖν fairly frequently (note especially the "meeting" of the two terms in 6.13 and 11.15). He thus draws our attention to the question of the relation of knowing and doing. He indicates his answer by the synonymous use of βέλτιον εἰδέναι and μᾶλλον εἰδέναι in the opening passage (1.1-2; observe the density of εἰδέναι). Knowledge is intrinsically good, whereas action is not (cf. Plato, *Gorgias* 467e ff.): to know to a greater degree is to know better, whereas to do to a greater degree is not necessarily to "do" better. Κακῶς ποιεῖν is as much ποιεῖν as is εὖ ποιεῖν whereas κακῶς εἰδέναι is practically identical with not knowing at all. (See *Cyropaedia* III 3.9 and II 3.13).

³⁶ *Hiero* 9.9-10. The opposite view is stated by Isocrates in his *To Nicocles* 17.

³⁷ The distinction suggested by Simonides between the wise and the rulers reminds one of Socrates' distinction between his own pursuit which consists in making people capable of political action on the one hand, and political activity proper on the other (*Memorabilia* I 6.15). According to Socrates, the specific understanding required of the ruler is not identical with wisdom strictly speaking. (Compare the explicit definition of wisdom in *Memorabilia* IV 6.7 — see also *ib.* 6.1 and I 1.16 — with the explicit definition of rule in III 9.10-13 where the term "wisdom" is studiously avoided.) In accordance with this, Xenophon hesitates to speak of the wisdom of either of the two Cyrus's, and when calling Agesilaus "wise," he evidently uses the term in a loose sense, not to say in the vulgar sense (*Agesilaus* 6.4-8 and 11.9). In the *Cyropaedia*, he adumbrates the relation between the ruler and the wise man by the conversations between Cyrus on the one hand, his father (whose manner of speaking is reminiscent of that of Socrates) and Tigranes (the pupil of a sophist whose fate is reminiscent of the fate of Socrates) on the other. Compare pp. 13 and 48 above. Compare IV, note 50 above.

³⁸ See pp. 39-40 above. Compare Plato, *Republic* 620c3-d2.

³⁹ See p. 21 above. Compare Plato, *Republic* 581e6-582e9.

⁴⁰ "Honor *seems* to be something great" and "no human pleasure *seems* to come nearer to divinity than the enjoyment connected with honors." (*Hiero* 7.1, 4). See also the ὡς ἔοικε in 7.2 and the εἰκότως δοκεῖτε in 7.4. Compare III b, note 41 above.

⁴¹ Since the preferences of a wise man are wise, we may say that Simonides reveals his wisdom in his statement on honor to a much higher degree than in his preceding utterances. The effect of that statement on Hiero would therefore ultimately be due to the fact that through it he faces Simonides' wisdom for the first time in the conversation. Without doubt, he interprets Simonides' wisdom, at least to begin with, in accordance with his own view—the vulgar view—of wisdom. Compare note 12 above.

⁴² ἐμφύεται. . . ἐμφύῃ (*Hiero* 7.3). Compare *Cyropaedia* I 2.1-2 and *Oeconomicus* 13.9.

⁴³ In *Hiero* 8.5-6 (as distinguished from *ib.* 7.1-4) Simonides does not suggest that rulers are honored more than private men. He does not say that only rulers, and not private men, are honored by the gods (cf. *Apol. Socr* 14-18). He says that a given individual is honored more highly when being a ruler than when living as a private man; he does not exclude the possibility that that individual is in all circumstances less honored than another man who never rules. In the last part of 8.5 he replaces "ruler" by the more general "those honored above others" (cf. *Apol. Socr.* 21). The bearing

of 8.6 is still more limited as appears from a comparison of the passage with 2.1 and 7.3. — Love of honor may seem to be characteristic of those wise men who converse with tyrants. Plato's Socrates says of Simonides that he was desirous of honor in regard to wisdom (*Protagoras* 343b7-c3).

44 *Hiero* 3.1, 6, 8. Compare *ib.* 1.19, 21-23, 29 and 4.8. See III b, note 34 above.

45 Compare *Hiero* 3.1-9 with *ib.* 8.1 and 11.8 (the emphatic "you"). See also Hiero's last utterance in 10.1. Hiero's praise of honor in 7.9-10 is clearly not spontaneous but solicited by Simonides' praise of honor in 7.1-4. Hiero's praise of honor differs from Simonides' in this, that only according to the former is love a necessary element of honor. Furthermore, it should be noted that Hiero makes a distinction between pleasure and the satisfaction of ambition (1.27). Xenophon's characterisation of Hiero does not contradict the obvious fact that the tyrant is desirous of honors (cf. 4.6 as well as the emphasis on Hiero's concern with being loved with Aristotle's analysis in *Eth. Nic.* 1159a12 ff.). But Xenophon asserts by implication that the tyrant's, or the ruler's, desire for honor is inseparable from the desire for being loved by human beings. — The most obvious explanation of the fact that Hiero stresses "love" and Simonides stresses "honor" would of course be this: Hiero stresses the things which the tyrant lacks, whereas Simonides stresses the things which the tyrant enjoys. Now, tyrants are commonly hated (cf. Aristotle, *Politics* 1312b19-20) but they are honored. This explanation is correct but insufficient because it does not account for Simonides' genuine concern with honor or praise and for his genuine indifference to being loved by human beings.

46 Compare *Hiero* 7.1-4 with *ib.* 1.16 and the passages cited in the preceding note. The forms of honor other than praise and admiration partake of the characteristic features of love rather than of those of praise and admiration. The fact that Simonides speaks in the crucial passage (*Hiero* 7.1-4) of honor in general, is due to his adaptation to Hiero's concern with love. Consider also the emphasis on honor rather than on praise in ch. 9.

47 Plato, *Gorgias* 481d4-5 and 513c7-8. Compare also the characterization of the tyrant in the *Republic* (see III b, note 12 above). As regards the disagreement between Hiero and Simonides concerning the status of "human beings," compare the disagreement between the politician and the philosopher on the same subject in Plato's *Laws* (804b5-c1).

48 This explains also the different attitude of the two types to envy. See p. 70 above.

49 Compare Plato, *Gorgias* 481d4-5.

50 *Hiero* 11.8-15. Compare *Agesilaus* 6.5 and 11.15.

51 *Hiero* 7.9. Compare Plato, *Republic* 330c3-6 and *Laws* 873c2-4; Aristotle, *Politics* 1262b22-24. Compare also p. 14 and II, note 22 above. — Cf. 1 Peter 1.8 and Cardinal Newman's comment: "St. Peter makes it almost a description of the Christian, that he loves whom he has not seen."

52 Simonides fr. 99 Bergk.

53 Cf. the use of φίλοι in the sense of fellow-citizens as opposed to strangers or enemies in *Hiero* 11.15, *Memorabilia* I 3.3, and *Cyropaedia* II 2.15.

54 *Hiero* 8.1-7. That this is not the last word of Xenophon on love, appears most clearly from *Oeconomicus* 20.29.

55 Compare *Hiero* 7.9 and 11.14-15 with *Hellenica* VII 3.12 (*Cyropaedia* III 3.4) and *Memorabilia* IV 8.7. The popular view is apparently adopted in Aristotle's *Politics* 1286b11-12 (cf. 1310b33 ff.). Compare Plato, *Gorgias* 513e5 ff. and 520e7-11.

114   ON TYRANNY

56 Compare *Hiero* 7.9 with *ib.* 7.1-4.

57 Men of excellence in an emphatic sense are Hesiod, Epicharmus and Prodicus (*Memorabilia* II 1.20-21). Compare also *Memorabilia* I 4.2-3 and 6.14.

58 *Memorabilia* I 2.3 and 6.10. — Simonides' statement that no human pleasure seems to come nearer to the divine than the enjoyment connected with honors (*Hiero* 7.4) is ambiguous. In particular, it may refer to the belief that the very gods derive pleasure from being honored (whereas they presumably do not enjoy the other pleasures discussed in the dialogue) or it may refer to the connection between the highest ambition and god-like self-sufficiency. Compare VI, note 6 below.

59 As for the connection between this kind of selfishness and wisdom, compare Plato, *Gorgias* 458a2-7 and the definition of justice in the *Republic*. — Considerations which were in one respect similar to those indicated in our text seem to have induced Hegel to abandon his youthful "dialectics of love" in favor of the "dialectics of the desire for recognition." See A. Kojève, *Introduction à l'étude de Hegel*, Paris (Gallimard), 1947, 187 and 510-512, and the same author's "Hegel, Marx et le Christianisme," *Critique*, 1946, 350-352.

60 Compare Simonides' disparaging remark on a kind of pleasure which is enjoyed by others rather than by oneself in *Hiero* 1.24 (cf. III b, note 11 above). Consider also the ambiguity of "food" (*Memorabilia* III 5.10; Plato, *Protagoras* 313c5-7). — As regards the connection between friendship ("love") and sex, cf. *Hiero* 1.33, 36-38 and 7.6. — The explanation suggested in the text can easily be reconciled with the fact that Hiero's concern with the pleasures of sex, if taken literally, would seem to characterize him, not as a ruler in general, but as an imperfect ruler. Xenophon's most perfect ruler, the older Cyrus, is characterized by the almost complete absence of concern with such pleasures. What is true of the perfect ruler, is still more true of the wise: whereas Cyrus does not dare to look at the beautiful Panthea, Socrates visits the beautiful Theodote without any hesitation (cf *Cyropaedia* V 1.7 ff. with *Memorabilia* III 11.1; *Memorabilia* I 2.1 and 3.8-15; *Oeconomicus* 12.13-14; *Agesilaus* 5.4-5). To use the Aristotelian terms, whereas Cyrus is continent, Socrates is temperate or moderate. In other words, Cyrus' temperance is combined with inability or unwillingness to look at the beautiful or to admire it (cf. *Cyropaedia* V 1.8 and VIII 1.42), whereas Socrates' temperance is the foundation for his ability and willingness to look at the beautiful and to admire it. To return to Hiero, he reveals a strong interest in the pleasures of sight (*Hiero* 1.11-13; cf. 11.10). He is concerned not so much with the pleasures of sex in general as with those of homosexuality. This connects him somehow with Socrates: love of men seems to bespeak a higher aspiration than love of women. (*Symposium* 8.2, 29; *Cyropaedia* II 2.28; Plato, *Symposium* 208d ff. Cf. Montesquieu, *De l'esprit des lois* VII 9 note: "Quant au vrai amour, dit Plutarque, les femmes n'y ont aucune part. Il parlait comme son siècle. Voyez Xénophon, au dialogue intitulé *Hiéron*.") Hiero is presented as a ruler who is capable of conversing with the wise and of appreciating them (cf. III a, note 44 above). Does Hiero's education explain why he is not a perfect ruler? Only the full understanding of the education of Cyrus would enable one to answer this question. — Compare IV, note 50 above.

61 *Hiero* 11.7, 11-15. *Memorabilia* I 2.11.

62 *Hiero* 6.9. — How little Simonides impresses Hiero, a good judge in this matter, as being warlike, is indicated by the latter's "*if* you too have experience of war" (6.7) as compared with his "I know well that you too

have experience" regarding the pleasures of the table (1.19). Cf. also *ib.*
1.29, 23. — Consider Simonides' silence about "manliness" (p. 48 above),
and compare III b, notes 18 and 38, and III c, note 6 above.
[63] *Hiero* 11.7. In the parallel in the *Agesilaus* (9.7) the qualifying
words "among human beings" are omitted.
[64] *Hiero* 2.7-18. (Consider the conditional clauses in 2.7.) The emphasis
in this passage is certainly on war. The passage consists of two parts: In the
first part (2.7-11) in which Hiero shows that if peace is good and war bad,
tyrants are worse off than private citizens, "peace" occurs three times and
"war" (and derivations) seven times; in the second part (2.12-18) in which
he shows that as regards the pleasures of war — or more specifically as regards the pleasures of wars waged against forcibly subjected people, i.e.,
against rebellious subjects — tyrants are worse off than private citizens,
"peace" does not occur at all but "war" (and derivatives) occurs seven
times.
[65] Plato, *Republic* 566e6-567a9. Aristotle, *Politics* 1313b28-30 and
1305a18-22.
[66] *Cyropaedia* I 4.24; VII 1.13. *Memorabilia* III 1.6. Compare Plato,
Republic 375c1-2 and 537a6-7 with Aristotle, *Politics* 1327b38-1328a11.
[67] *Hiero* 1.34-35. As regards the relation between Eros and Ares, compare
Simonides fr. 43 Bergk and Aristotle, *Politics* 1269b24-32.
[68] *Hiero* 6.5; compare *ib.* 6.14.
[69] *Hiero* 2.2; 6.12-14. Compare the use of the second person singular in
6.13 on the one hand, and in 6.14 on the other.
[70] *Hiero* 5.1. *Apol. Socr.* 16. *Memorabilia* I 6.10. Socrates does not teach
strategy whereas he does teach economics (compare *Memorabilia* III 1 and
IV 7.1 with the *Oeconomicus*). Compare Plato, *Republic* 366c7-d1 and the
passages indicated in IV, note 45 above.

VI. PLEASURE AND VIRTUE

[1] Compare *Memorabilia* IV 8.11.
[2] See pp. 25-28 and III a, note 44 above.
[3] Compare *Hiero* 8.6 with *ib.* 2.1 and 7.3. Compare *Hiero* 5.1-2 with *ib.*
3.1-9 and 6.1-3 on the one hand, and with *Memorabilia* II 4 and I 6.14 on
the other. Compare *Hiero* 1.11-14 with *Memorabilia* II 1.31: Hiero does
not mention one's own virtuous actions as the most pleasant sight. Compare
Hiero 3.2 with *Symposium* 8.18: he does not mention the common enjoyment of friends about their noble actions among the pleasures of friendships.
He replaces Simonides' ἐπινοεῖν by ἐπιθυμεῖν (*Hiero* 2.2 and 4.7).
[4] *Hiero* 7.9-10.
[5] Aristotle's suggestions for the improvement of tyrannical government
(in the fifth book of the *Politics*) are more akin in spirit to Xenophon's
suggestions than to Isocrates'; they are, however, somewhat more moralistic
than those made in the *Hiero*.
[6] Fr. 71 Bergk. — When Xenophon's Simonides says that no human
pleasure seems to come nearer to the divine than the enjoyment connected
with honors, he may imply that "the divine" is pure pleasure. Compare V,
note 58 above.
[7] Compare *Hiero* 4.10 with frs. 5, 38, 39 and 42 Bergk. Compare Plato,
Protagoras 346b5-8. — Compare also Simonides' definition of nobility as old
wealth with Aristotle's view according to which it is not so much wealth as
virtue that is of the essence of nobility (*Politics* 1255a32 ff., 1283a33-38,
1301b3-4).

8 *Lyra Graeca*, ed. by J. M. Edmonds, vol. 2, revised and augmented edition, 258. Compare p. 48 above. See *Hellenica* II 3.19 and *Apol. Socr.* 30.

9 *Lyra Graeca*, ed. *cit.*, 250, 256 and 260. Compare Plato, *Protagoras* 316d3-7, 338e6 ff. and 340e9 ff.; also *Republic* 331e1-4 and context (Simonides did not say that to say the truth is of the essence of justice).

10 Compare pp. 13, 20, 33, 35, 37-38, and 62 above.

11 Compare pp. 74 ff. above.

12 This would also explain why Simonides emphasizes somewhat later on the pleasures connected with food: food is the fundamental need of all animals (*Memorabilia* II 1.1). In *Hiero* 7.3, where he hides his wisdom to a lesser degree than in the preceding sections, he does not call, as he did in 2.1, the pleasures of the body "small things."

13 Compare *Memorabilia* I 4.5 and IV 3.11.

14 Compare Plato, *Theaetetus* 184c5-7 and 185e6-7.

15 *Hiero* 1.1. Compare the κάλλιον θεᾶσθαι in 2.3 with the ἥδιον θεᾶσθαι in 8.6.

16 *Hiero* 1.5. A remark which Simonides makes later on (9.10) might induce one to believe that he identified the good with the useful, and this might be thought to imply that the end for which the good things are useful, is pleasure. This interpretation would not take account of the facts which we discuss in the text. Simonides must therefore be presumed to have distinguished between the good which is good because it is useful for something else, and the good which is intrinsically good and not identical with the pleasant.

17 *Hiero* 1.22.

18 *Hiero* 1.9; 2.1; 7.3.

19 See the reference to the divine in *Hiero* 7.4.

20 *Hiero* 1.27; 3.3; 6.16.

21 The importance of the problem "fatherland-friendship" for the understanding of the *Hiero* is shown by the fact that that problem determines the plan of the bulk of the second section (ch. 3-6). This is the plan of ch. 3-6: I a) friendship (3.1-9); b) trust (4.1-2); c) fatherland (4.3-5). II a) possessions (4.6-11); b) good men or the virtuous (5.1-2); c) fatherland (5.3-4). III a) pleasures of private men (6.1-3); b) fear, protection, laws (6.4-11); c) helping friends and hurting enemies (6.12-15). The difference between "fatherland" and "trust" is not as clear-cut as that between either of them and "friendship": both fatherland and trust are good with regard to protection, or freedom from fear, whereas friendship is intrinsically pleasant. "Friendship" can be replaced by "possessions" for the reason given in *Hiero* 3.6, *Memorabilia* II 4.3-7 and *Oeconomicus* 1.14; "friendship" can be replaced by "pleasures of private men" for the reason given in *Hiero* 6.1-3. "Trust" can be replaced by "virtue" (cf. Plato, *Laws* 630b2-c6) as well as by "protection" (trustworthiness is the specific virtue of guards: *Hiero* 6.11). "Fatherland" can be replaced by "helping the friends and hurting the enemies" with a view to the fact that helping the friends, i.e., the fellow-citizens, and hurting the enemies, i.e., the enemies of the city, is the essence of patriotism (cf. *Symposium* 8.38). The same distinction which governs the plan of ch. 3-6, governs the plan of ch. 8-11 as well: a) friendship (ch. 8-9; see 10.1); b) protection (guards) (ch. 10); c) fatherland or city (ch. 11; see 11.1).

22 Compare *Hiero* 3.3 with 4.1 on the one hand, and with 4.3-5 on the other. Compare 4.2 and 6.11.

23 *Hiero* 4.3-4. Compare 6.6, 10. In what may best be called the repetition of the statement on the fatherland (5.3-4), Hiero says that it is neces-

sary to be patriotic because one cannot be preserved or be happy without the city. Compare the οὐκ ἄνευ in 5.3 with the (οὐκ) ἄνευ in 4.1. From 5.3-4 it appears that the power and renown of the fatherland is normally pleasant. When speaking of friendship, Hiero had not spoken of the power and renown of friends: he had not implied that only powerful and renowned friends are pleasant (compare *Agesilaus* 10.3). Not the fatherland, but power and renown are pleasant, and the power and renown of one's city are pleasant because they contribute to one's own power and renown. Compare *Hiero* 11.13. — When speaking of the pleasures which he enjoyed while being a private man, Hiero mentions friendship; he does not mention the city or the fatherland (6.1-3).

24 *Hiero* 4.3-4 and 5.3.

25 Compare *Hiero* 4.3 and 10.4 with 6.10.

26 *Hiero* 9.2-4 (cf. 1.37; 5.2-3; 8.9). Compare also Hiero's emphasis (in his statement on friendship: 3.7-9) on the relations within the family, with the opposite emphasis in Xenophon's account of Socrates' character (*Memorabilia* II 2-10): the blood relations are "necessary" (*Memorabilia* II 1.14). *Cyropaedia* IV 2.11. *Anabasis* VII 7.29. *Memorabilia* II 1.18. Compare Aristotle, *Rhetoric* 1370a8-17 and Empedocles fr. 116 (Diels, *Vorsokratiker,* first ed.). See V, note 27 above.

27 Compare *Hiero* 5.3 and 4.9 with 3.1-9.

28 Observe that friendship and virtue occur in different columns of the plan of ch. 3-6 (see note 21 above). Compare Hiero's praise of the friend with Socrates' praise of the good friend (*Memorabilia* II 4 and 6).

29 *Hiero* 11.14.

30 *Hiero* 11.1, 5-6. Compare pp. 74 ff. above.

31 Compare *Hellenica* I 7.21.

32 Compare *Hiero* 4.3 with *Memorabilia* II 3.2 and 1.13-15.

33 Only the fairly short first part of the *Memorabilia* (I 1-2) deals with "Socrates and the city," whereas the bulk of the work deals with "Socrates' character"; see the two perorations: I 2.62-64 and IV 8.11. — As regards the plan of the *Memorabilia,* see Emma Edelstein, *Xenophontisches und Platonisches Bild des Sokrates,* Berlin, 1935, 78-137.

34 Isocrates, *Antidosis* 155-156.

35 *Anabasis* III 1.4-9; V 6.15-37. Compare *ib.* V 3.7 and VII 7.57. — The sentiment of Proxenus is akin to that expressed by Hermes in Aristophanes' *Plutus* 1151 (*Ubi bene ibi patria*). (Compare *Hiero* 5.1 and 6.4 with *Plutus* 1 and 89.) Compare Cicero, *Tusc. disput.* V 37.106 ff.

36 *Anabasis* V 3.6 and *Hellenica* IV 3.15 (cf. IV 2.17).

37 B. G. Niebuhr, "Ueber Xenophons Hellenika," *Kleine historische und philosophische Schriften,* I, Bonn, 1828, 467: "Wahrlich einen ausgearteteren Sohn hat kein Staat jemals ausgestossen als diesen Xenophon. Plato war auch kein guter Bürger, Athens wert war er nicht, unbegreifliche Schritte hat er getan, er steht wie ein Sünder gegen die Heiligen, Thukydides und Demosthenes, aber doch wie ganz anders als dieser alte Tor!"

38 *Hiero* 4.3-5 and 5.3.

39 See p. 61 above.

40 *Cyropaedia* II 2.24-26. Dakyns comments on the passage as follows: "Xenophon's breadth of view: virtue is not confined to citizens, but we have the pick of the whole world. Cosmopolitan Hellenism." Consider the conditional clauses in *Agesilaus* 7.4, 7. Compare *Hipparchicus* 9.6 and *De vectigalibus* 2.1-5.

41 Compare Burke, *Reflections on the Revolution in France,* Everyman's Library ed., p. 59, on the one hand, and Pascal, *Provinciables* XIII as well as

Kant, "Über den Gemeinspruch: Das mag in the Theorie richtig sein, taugt aber nicht für die Praxis," on the other.

[42] Socrates' statement that cities and nations are "the wisest of human things" (*Memorabilia* I 4.16) does not mean then that the collective wisdom of political societies is superior to the wisdom of wise individuals. The positive meaning of the statement cannot be established but by detailed interpretation of the conversation during which the statement is made.

[43] The only special virtues of which Simonides speaks with some emphasis, are moderation and justice. Moderation may be produced by fear, the spoiler of all pleasures (*Hiero* 10.2-3 and 6.6; cf. IV, note 35 above), and it goes along with lack of leisure (9.8). As for justice, Simonides speaks once of a special kind of justice, the justice in business relations, and twice of "doing injustice" (9.6 and 10.8). Now, the term "justice" designates in Xenophon's works a variety of kindred phenomena which range from the most narrow legalism to the confines of pure and universal beneficence. Justice may be identical with moderation, it may be a subdivision of moderation, and it may be a virtue apart from moderation. It is certain that Simonides does not understand by justice legality, and there is no reason to suppose that he identified justice with beneficence. He apparently holds a considerably more narrow view of justice than does Hiero. (For Hiero's view of justice, see especially 5.1-2 and 4.11.) He replaces Hiero's "unjust men" by "those who commit unjust actions" (for the interpretation consider Aristotle, *Eth. Nic.* 1134a17 ff.). Whereas Hiero identifies justice and moderation by using ἀδικεῖν and ὑβρίζειν synonymously, Simonides distinguishes the two virtues from each other: he identifies ἀδικεῖν and κακουργεῖν and he distinguishes between κακουργεῖν with ὑβρίζειν (see 8.9; 9.8; 10.8, 2-4; cf. Aristotle, *Rhetoric* 1389b7-8 and 1390a17-18; Plato, *Protagoras* 326a4-5). It seems that Simonides understands by justice the abstaining from harming others (cf. *Agesilaus* 11.8 and *Memorabilia* IV 4.11-12; consider *Symposium* 4.15) and that he thus makes allowance for the problem inherent in benefiting "human beings" (as distinguished from "real men" or "men of excellence"). It is easy to see that justice thus understood, as distinguished from its motives and results, is not intrinsically pleasant.

[44] *Memorabilia* II 1.23, 26, 29.

[45] Diogenes Laertius II 65-66.

[46] Compare *Memorabilia* II 1.34 with *ib.* I 6.13, *Symposium* 1.5 and 4.62 and *Cynegeticus* 13.

[47] *Memorabilia* I 3.8-13.

[48] Compare *Hiero* 11.15 with *Anabasis* VII 7.41. See *Anabasis* II 1.12 (cf. Simonides fr. 5 Bergk) and *Cyropaedia* I 5.8-10; also *Agesilaus* 10.3.

[49] V. Brochard, *Études de philosophie ancienne et de philosophie moderne,* Paris (Vrin), 1926, 43.

[50] Compare III a, note 27 and IV, note 25 above.

[51] *Memorabilia* IV 6. 15.

[52] *Memorabilia* IV 8.6-8 (cf. I 6.9 and IV 5.9-10). *Apol. Socr.* 5-6 and 32.

[53] Compare Plato, *Republic* 357b4-358a3.

[54] *Apol. Socr.* 5. Compare *Memorabilia* II 1.19. Regarding *sibi ipsi placere* see especially Spinoza, *Ethics* III, aff. deff. 25. As for the difference between Socrates and Simonides, compare also p. 82 above.

VII. PIETY AND LAW

[1] *De vectigalibus* 6.2-3. Compare pp. 10-11 above.

[2] When Simonides suggests to Hiero that he should spend money for the

adornment of his city with temples *inter alia* (*Hiero* 11.1-2), he does not admonish him to practice piety; he merely advises him to spend his money in a way proper to a ruler. Aristotle's ethics which is silent about piety, mentions expenses for the worship of the gods under the heading "munificence." (*Eth. Nic.* 1122b19-23. Compare *Politics* 1321a35 ff. Cf. also J. F. Gronovius' note to Grotius' *De jure belli ac pacis*, Prolegg. §45: "Aristoteli ignoscendum, si inter virtutes morales non posuit religionem. . . . Nam illi ut veteribus omnibus extra Ecclesiam cultus deorum sub magnificentia ponitur.")

3 *Agesilaus* 1.34 and *Anabasis* III 2.13. Compare Plato, *Republic* 573c3-6.

4 *Politics* 1314b39 ff. No remark of this kind occurs in Aristotle's discussion of the preservation of the other régimes in the fifth book of the *Politics*. — *Cyropaedia* VIII 1.23. Compare Isocrates, *To Nicocles* 20 and Machiavelli, *Principe* XVIII.

5 *Memorabilia* IV 6.2-4.

6 *Memorabilia* IV 8.11; I 4; IV 3.

7 *Hiero* 3.9. Compare *Oeconomicus* 7.16, 29-30 (cf. 7.22-28).

8 Cicero, *De natura deorum* I 22.60.

9 Φύσις and φύειν (or derivatives) occur in *Hiero* 1.22, 31, 33; 3.9; 7.3; 9.8. θεοί occurs in 3.5; 4.2; 8.5. Τὸ θεῖον occurs in 7.4. Compare the remarks on ἱερά in 4.5, 11 with *Hellenica* VI 4.30.

10 Compare *Anabasis* V 2.24-25 and Plato, *Laws* 709b7-8. — Considering the relation between "nature" and "truth" (*Oeconomicus* 10.2 and *Memorabilia* II 1.22), the distinction between nature and law may imply the view that the law necessarily contains fictitious elements. In *Hiero* 3.3 Hiero says: "It has not even escaped the cities that friendship is a very great good and most pleasant to human beings. At any rate, many cities have a law (νομίζουσι) that only adulterers may be killed with impunity, evidently for this reason, because they believe (νομίζουσι) that they (the adulterers) are the destroyers of the wives' friendship with their husbands." The law that adulterers may be killed with impunity is based on the belief that the adulterers as distinguished from the wives are responsible for the wives' faithlessness. The question arises whether this belief is always sound. Xenophon alludes to this difficulty by making Hiero take up the question of the possible guilt of the wife in the subsequent sentence: "Since when the wife has been raped, husbands do not honor their wives any less on that account, provided the wives' love remains inviolate." It seems that the men's belief in the modesty of women is considered conducive to that modesty. Compare Montesquieu, *De l'esprit des lois* VI 17: "Parce que les hommes sont méchants, la loi est obligée de les supposer meilleurs qu'ils ne sont. Ainsi . . . on juge . . . que tout enfant conçu pendant le mariage est légitime; la loi a confiance en la mère comme si elle était la pudicité même." Cf. also Rousseau, *Émile* V (ed. Garnier, vol. 2, 147-148) — Similarly, by considering (νομίζων) one's sons as the same thing as one's life or soul (*Hiero* 11.14), whereas in truth one's sons are not one's life or soul, one will be induced to act more beneficently than one otherwise would.

11 *Anabasis* II 6.19-20 (cf. Aristotle, *Eth. Nic.* 1179b4 ff.). *Symposium* 4.19.

INDEX

Alcmæon, 102.
Antisthenes, 70.
Aristippus, 89, 90.
Aristophanes, 96, 117.
Aristotle, 59, 93, 95, 96, 97, 98, 99, 101, 102, 103, 105, 106, 107, 108, 109, 110, 111, 113, 114, 115, 117, 118, 119.
Brochard, Victor, 118.
Burke, 109, 117.
Burnet, John, 109.
Cicero, 5, 95, 105, 117, 119.
Dakyns, H. G., 117.
Diodorus Siculus, 101.
Diogenes Laertius, 118.
Edelstein, Emma, 117.
Empedocles, 117.
Epicharmus, 114.
Euripides, 95.
Gorgias, 87.
Gronovius, J. F., 119.
Grote, George, 96.
Hegel, 114.
Hesiod, 114.
Hippodamus, 109.
Hirzel, Rudolf, 101, 110.
Hobbes, 95.
Homer, 28.
Hume, 108.
Isocrates, 81, 95, 96, 97, 101, 111, 112, 115, 117, 119.
Kant, 118.
Kojève, Alexandre, 114.
Lessing, 96.

Lincke, K., 104, 106.
Livy, 5.
Macaulay, IX, 104.
Machiavelli, 2, 3, 38, 47, 54, 95, 107, 108, 119.
Marchant, E. C., 101, 102, 103, 104, 107.
Montesquieu, 95, 107, 108, 114, 119.
Newman, Cardinal, 113.
Niebuhr, B. G., 117.
Pascal, 117.
Peter, The First Epistle of, 113.
Pindar, 98, 106.
Plato, 1, 5, 6, 52, 62, 74, 75, 90, 91, 95, 96, 97, 98, 99, 100, 101, 102, 105, 106, 107, 108, 109, 110, 111, 112, 113, 114, 115, 116, 118, 119.
Polos, 52.
Prodicus, 89, 114.
Richter, Ernst, 100, 107.
Rousseau, 107, 119.
Samuel, The Second Book of, 106.
Socrates, 3, 5, 6, 9, 10, 11, 12, 13, 16, 17, 22, 23, 28, 31, 44, 51, 52, 56, 57, 58, 59, 60, 61, 62, 63, 64, 68, 70, 71, 72, 73, 74, 75, 79, 86, 87, 88, 90, 91, 92, 93, 94, 98, 100, 103, 107, 111, 112, 113, 114, 115, 117, 118.
Spinoza, 118.
Thrasymachus, 52.
Thucydides, 5, 100.
Voltaire, 96.

Printed in U.S.A.
by
Futuro Press, New York City 200